Jean Baudrillard

Core Cultural Theorists

Core Cultural Theorists is the first book series in cultural theory to be aimed at the interests and needs of Cultural Studies students. It aims to give concise, critically informed guides to the seminal thinkers in the study of culture.

Jean Baudrillard

The Defence of the Real

Rex Butler

SAGE Publications
London • Thousand Oaks • New Delhi

With thanks to Nicholas Zurbrugg

© Rex Butler 1999

First published 1999

 SAGE Publications Ltd
6 Bonhill Street
London EC2A 4PU

SAGE Publications Inc.
2455 Teller Road
Thousand Oaks, California 91320

SAGE Publications India Pvt Ltd
32, M-Block Market
Greater Kailash – I
New Delhi 110 048

British Library Cataloguing in Publication data

A catalogue record for this book is available
from the British Library

ISBN 0 7619 5832 0
ISBN 0 7619 5833 9 (pbk)

Library of Congress catalog card number

Typeset by Mayhew Typesetting, Rhayader, Powys
Printed in Great Britain by Biddles Ltd, Guildford Surrey

Contents

Abbreviations

The following texts of Baudrillard are indicated by initials. The existing English translations have been used wherever possible, although they have occasionally been modified. Where no English version exists, we have translated it ourselves. In these cases, both here and in the References, we have included the original French title after our English equivalent.

'BE'   'The Beaubourg Effect: Implosion and Dissuasion', *October* 20, 1982: 1–13

BL   *Baudrillard Live: Selected Interviews*, ed. Mike Gane (London: Routledge, 1993)

CM I   *Cool Memories I* (London: Verso, 1990)

CM II *Cool Memories II* (Paris: Galilée, 1990)

CS   *Consumer Society* [*La société de consommation*] (Paris: Denoël, 1970)

EC   *The Ecstasy of Communication* (New York: Semiotext(e), 1988)

ED   *The Evil Demon of Images* (Sydney: Power Publishing, 1988)

'FF'   'Forget Foucault' ['Oublier Foucault'] in *Theoretical Strategies* (Sydney: Local Consumption Publications, 1982): 188–214

'FM'	'Please Follow Me', *Art & Text* 23/4, 1987: 103–12
FS	*Fatal Strategies* (New York: Semiotext(e), 1990)
IE	*The Illusion of the End* (Cambridge: Polity Press, 1994)
MP	*The Mirror of Production* (St Louis, MO: Telos, 1975)
'OS'	'The Orders of Simulacra', in *Simulations* (New York: Semiotext(e), 1983): 81–159
PC	*The Perfect Crime* (London: Verso, 1996)
PE	*For a Critique of the Political Economy of the Sign* (St Louis, MO: Telos, 1981)
'PS'	'The Precession of Simulacra', in *Simulations* (New York: Semiotext(e), 1983): 1–79
S	*Seduction* (Montreal: New World Perspectives, 1990)
S and S	*Simulacra and Simulation [Simulacres et simulation]* (Paris: Galilée, 1981)
SE	*Symbolic Exchange and Death* (London: Sage Publications, 1993)
SO	*The System of Objects* (London: Verso, 1996)
SSM	*In the Shadow of the Silent Majorities* (New York: Semiotext(e), 1983)
TE	*The Transparency of Evil: Essays on Extreme Phenomena* (London: Verso, 1993)
'2000'	'The Year 2000 Will Not Take Place', in E.A. Grosz, T. Threadgold, D. Kelly, A. Cholodenko and E. Colless (eds), *Futur*Fall: Excursions into Postmodernity* (Sydney: Power Publishing, 1986): 18–28

Introduction:

Reading Baudrillard in His Own Terms

One of the world's major thinkers sits at a desk on stage in a casino some thirty miles south of Las Vegas. After being introduced to the audience, he waits for the applause to die down then leans over into the microphone and begins to read. He is there as part of a giant New Age festival entitled *Chance: Three Days in the Desert*, described as a 'rave and summit meeting between artists and philosophers, chaosophists and croupiers, mathematicians and musicians' (Hultkrans 1997: 21). About sixty-five years old, he is short, stocky, bespectacled, balding. A commentator at the event will even wonder, with his 'diminutive height, wine-and-cheese paunch, nose and self-rolled cigarettes', 'is there anyone more French than this man?' (1997: 22) Over the sound of slot machines being played and the occasional jackpot being won, the disparate group of listeners strains to catch what he is saying through his heavily accented English. 'Chaos' sounds like 'cows', 'bodies' like 'birdies'. Later in the evening, he will return to recite one of his poems, 'Motel Suicide', backed by a rock band and wearing a gold lamé suit. Despite complaining about the 'criminally pretentious' nature of his verse, the same commentator will nevertheless go on to praise him as a 'real trouper' (1997: 22). When he asks him the next morning why he does this sort of thing, he will laconically reply: 'curiosity', before going on to add something about 'confronting the indifference of the world' (1997: 22).

Who is this thinker who appears on stage in such strange circumstances and thereby risks falling into embarrassment, his words misunderstood by his followers or drowned beneath the noise of slot machines? Why does he tempt fate by speaking not only at a casino but amidst this absurd mélange of theorists, rock bands, performance artists and poets? How to reconcile his philosophy, which is profoundly unsentimental and anti-subjective, with what he has described as the 'soft ideology' (*CM I*, 22–3) of these techno-futurists and New Age travellers? Is he playing out the very collapse of the distinction between rationality and its other, the end of the Enlightenment project of making sense of the world, his work speaks of? Is he saying that even the most radical act of negation is destined to become merely another form of entertainment, indistinguishable from the average Las Vegas lounge act? Is he parodying himself as the empty token of an era now gone? Or is this on the contrary an opening up of himself to chance, the contingent, the objective rule of the world? Is this the kind of 'Stoic indifference' (*EC*, 101) he speaks about, discoursing in front of non-comprehending acolytes, many of whom would not have read his work, without which much of what he is saying would surely be incomprehensible, but who have only heard of his name? Is this act of appearing on stage with a rock band in a casino a repudiation of his philosophy or a confirmation of it?

The man under the spotlight is the French sociologist and cultural critic Jean Baudrillard, who in a series of books dating back to 1968 has charted our modern world and in a way the very situation that appeared to be unfolding up there on stage. Born in 1929 in the northern French city of Reims, he descends from a long line of peasants and is the first of his family to go to university. (Now he says, with characteristic humour: 'Generations of peasants worked hard all their lives: we owe it to them to make up for their expenditure with our own idleness' [*CM II*, 17].) At university, he studies German, then travels, then works as a secondary school teacher. During this time, he contributes a number of reviews to the journal *Les temps modernes*, established by Jean-Paul Sartre, on such authors as Italo Calvino, Uwe Johnson and William Styron. He also translates a series of important texts from German, including Bertolt Brecht's *Dialogue of the Exiles*, Peter Weiss's *Marat/Sade*, the social anthropologist Wilhelm Mühlmann's *Messianic Revolutionaries of the Third World* and Friedrich Engels's *The German Ideology*. He later returns to university to study sociology, and in 1966 completes his doctoral thesis, the passport to higher education teaching in France. He begins work at the Sociology Department of the University of Nanterre, Paris, that same year, where he is to remain for the remainder of his academic career. His thesis is published in slightly modified form in 1968 as his first book, *The System of Objects*. Inspired by the sociologist Henri Lefebvre's *Critique of Everyday Life* and the semiotician Roland Barthes's *Mythologies*, it attempts to discern the abstract 'language' that underlies our relationships with ordinary, domestic objects, arguing that we interact with them not so much in terms of their ostensible use value or function but as a way of communicating with others. He follows this up in 1970 with *Consumer Society*, which similarly wants to take what appears the most obvious and commonplace – human desires and needs – and show how they are produced both by and as a certain discourse within modern consumer society.

Baudrillard's next two books, *For a Critique of the Political Economy of the Sign* (1972) and *The Mirror of Production* (1973), are attempts to grapple with the weighty legacy of Marxism, an inevitable confrontation for any thinker with radical aspirations in France at the time. In the first, he seeks to demonstrate both that political economy is organized by a certain logic of the sign and that semiotics and structuralism, the two dominant 'sciences of the sign', rely upon a certain political economy. Baudrillard aims within the book to show how what he calls 'symbolic exchange' – a cyclical, reversible relationship between things – cuts against this political economy and any putative science of the sign. The non-linearity and reciprocality of symbolic exchange is opposed at once to the ideals of accumulation in political economy and communication and meaning in semiotics. This argument is continued in *The Mirror of Production*, in which Baudrillard accuses Marxism of sharing the same fundamental assumptions as that capitalism to which it is apparently opposed. Again, Marxism has no place for, or conception of symbolic exchange. And in his evocation of a 'primitive', non-rational economy here, Baudrillard is undoubtedly part of a wider movement of French intellectuals at the time rediscovering the work of the amateur anthropologist and author Georges Bataille and his notions of 'expenditure' and 'general' as opposed to 'restricted' economy. We would want to read Baudrillard at this point not only in the closest relationship with Bataille – something that has not really been done so far in the commentary on him[1] – but also with such other interpreters of Bataille as Jean-François Lyotard (*Pulsional Dispositions* and *Libidinal Economy*), Gilles Deleuze and Félix Guattari (*Anti-Oedipus* and *A Thousand Plateaus*) and Jacques Derrida (the essay 'From Restricted to General Economy: A Hegelianism Without Reserve' from the collection *Writing and Difference*, amongst others).

This first period of Baudrillard's theorizing comes to a head in the book *Symbolic Exchange and Death* (1976). At first sight an analysis of the place of death in contemporary Western society, it is in fact much more than this. It is a wide-ranging survey of symbolic exchange across a number of fields, its ambiguous status as both constitutive and deconstitutive of them. Baudrillard looks at the crisis surrounding production and labour in advanced capitalist countries, the linguist Ferdinand de Saussure's later work involving anagrams in classical Roman poetry, and Sigmund Freud's ambivalence regarding the concept of the death-drive in psychoanalysis and his study of the phenomena of jokes and slips of the tongue in ordinary language. The book is arguably Baudrillard's *magnum opus*, the definitive formulation and summing up of his ideas to this point, but it is also perhaps the last of his works of this kind. As he later admits ruefully in an interview: *Symbolic Exchange and Death* was the last book that inspired any confidence . . . Everything I write is deemed brilliant, intelligent, but not serious' (*BL*, 189). Why is this so? We will come back to it more fully in a moment, but *Symbolic Exchange and Death* is the last of Baudrillard's books that is observational, empirical, scientific. It is the last that comes out of his discipline, that could be taught in a conventional course in sociology. Death – although already it is a figure of speech, a trope for the more abstract and generalizable notion of symbolic exchange – is a real object, something that exists out there in the world before it is written about. It is a topic that can be measured, of which a history can be constructed, that is not simply a fabrication of Baudrillard himself. Henceforth, Baudrillard's work becomes fictional, inventive, 'pataphysical'. Criticism or theory understands itself no longer as responding to or explaining a previous real, but as bringing about its own real. Or Baudrillard's work engages with the real, but not in the way this is usually understood. It is a real not external but *internal* to the work. The model for Baudrillard's writing, though he rarely mentions him by name, is not the Marx, Freud or Saussure of before, but Nietzsche.

The first examples of this new type of approach are the essays 'The Beaubourg Effect: Implosion and Deterrence' and 'Forget Foucault', both of 1977. The former is a weird, almost science-fictional, attack upon Paris's famous Pompidou Centre, describing it as 'absorbing and devouring all cultural energy, rather like the black monolith of *2001: A Space Odyssey*'. The short polemic then concludes with an injunction not to avoid the museum but to flood it, make it collapse (literally) under the weight of its own success: 'Make Beaubourg buckle! A new revolutionary slogan. No need to torch it or to fight it. Just go there! That's the best way to destroy it' ('BE', 3). The latter is a subtle – and underrated – critique of the great French historian of madness, sexuality and institutionality, Michel Foucault. Here too, Baudrillard's argument appears unorthodox, perverted, deliberately paradoxical. He says that Foucault is wrong in his various studies not because he is empirically incorrect, but because he is *too* correct, *too* close to the truth:

> The very perfection of his [Foucault's] analytical chronicle of power is disquieting. Something tells us – but in the water- mark or the reverse side of this writing too fine to be true – that if it is possible after all to speak of power, sexuality, the body and discipline with this definitive intelligence, down to their most fragile metamorphoses, it is because, somewhere, all this is no longer relevant. (FF, 189)

These two essays are followed by *In the Shadow of the Silent Majorities* (1978), a text simultaneously of great interest to sociologists and an argument against the very possibility of sociology. After this, Baudrillard's work still perhaps relates to his original discipline, but only in an indirect way (the general question of how a theory operates, whether a physical or social science can ever be objective or empirical). The subject of *In the Shadow* is that nebulous sociological entity the 'masses', also known as the 'people'. The 'masses' are at once the most obvious and indisputable, the very basis of all sociology, and do not actually exist, are only a fiction produced by polls and surveys. They are what every political system and sociology tries to grasp – to ascertain their opinion, to educate, to represent – and what all inevitably fail to. The masses form an absolute limit to every sociology and theory of the social. Then, in 1979 Baudrillard publishes *Seduction*, a book that sees our lives ruled by the ineluctable destiny of what he calls 'seduction' – an 'ironic, alternative form that breaks with the referentiality of sex and provides a space, not of desire, but of play and defiance' (*S*, 21) – and that contains, amongst other things, a blistering attack upon much contemporary feminism for not seeing this, for reducing the relationship between the sexes to one of subservience/ dominance or biological difference. Three years later, Baudril- lard puts out *Simulacra and Simulation*, a collection of essays discussing his notion of 'simulation': the 'generation by models of a real without origin or reality, a hyperreal' ('PS', 3). Finally, in 1983 Baudrillard releases *Fatal Strategies*, in which he pushes to its furthest extent this series of idiosyncratic and provocative ideas he had been developing, some a continuation of that earlier concept of symbolic exchange and others an advance upon it: the masses, seduction, terrorism, the fatal, etc.

The years from *Symbolic Exchange and Death* in 1976 to *Fatal Strategies* in 1983 mark a period of frantic theoretical production (or seduction) for Baudrillard. They are the years when he first comes to prominence both in France and (especially) in such English-speaking countries as America, Britain and Australia. They are the years we would classify as constituting the second period in his career. As we suggest, during this time his work breaks away from the empirical, academic and sociological emphasis of the first period and envisages a different role for theory and criticism. If in the first period there is a critique of the scientific, systematizing pretensions of Marxism, psychoanalysis and semiotics, here in this second period this critique is put into practice. Baudrillard no longer claims to be impartial, objective, to offer a version of the truth. On the contrary, his work draws attention to its own fictionality, ingeniousness, singularity. Or, if a certain notion of truth does persist in it, it must be understood in a radically new sense, what Baudrillard calls the 'evident' as opposed to the 'true' (*CM II*, 34; *BL*, 179). Baudrillard begins to wonder in these works – a profound question for all French intellectuals after the failure of May '68 – what is the continued possibility of criticism, of theory, of the intellectual him- or herself? How are these able to change or transform the world? In what sense do the various Grand Narratives (Freedom, Rationality, Human Progress) that formerly guided revolutionary practice still apply? How to think and criticize in the absence of these?

After this, we see perhaps a different Baudrillard from before. In a way, a feeling of *ennui*, of stepping back from conclusions previously reached, marks the next phase of his career. In the journal *Cool Memories I*, compiled during this time, Baudrillard admits: 'It is possible that I have written the one – or two – best books I shall ever write. They are done with. That is how things go' (*CM I*, 3). Similarly, in an interview with the critic Sylvère Lotringer, Baudrillard speaks of how, after a certain point, he could no longer live with the theories he had developed: 'The giddiness I'm talking about ended up taking hold of me. I stopped working on simulation. I felt I was going totally mad' (*BL*, 105). If in his first period Baudrillard questioned science but was still scientific, and in his second period questioned theory but was still theoretical, now in this third period he gives up even the ambition to do theory. In 1987 too, Baudrillard leaves his teaching position at Nanterre, and this undoubtedly contributes to his sense of retirement, of being on what he describes as a permanent 'sabbatical' (*CM I*, 232). Baudrillard henceforth writes in a variety of genres, experimenting with form to a degree he never had before. There are no longer the extended scholarly treatises of the first period, or even the short essays and pamphlets of the second, but the travelogue of *America* (1986), the journals *Cool Memories I, II* and *III* (1987, 1990, 1996), the newspaper articles *The Gulf War Did Not Take Place* (1991) and even the loose survey of his own work in his *habilitation* thesis, *The Ecstasy of Communication* (1987), originally titled – beware the auto-biographical impulse in Baudrillard – in a parody of the well-known French series in which a leading intellectual is invited to look back over their career in the form *X by Him-* or *Herself, The Other by Itself*. Of late, Baudrillard has returned with a number of more conventionally structured books, composed of mini-chapters or fragments, though still written in this recent funereal or twilight mode: *The Transparency of Evil* (1990), *The Illusion of the End* (1992) and *The Perfect Crime* (1994).

In many ways, it is hard – and possibly even unnecessary – to summarize the arguments of this later period of Baudrillard's production. To a large extent, they are a continuation of what comes before. There is undeniably a sense, as opposed to the sustained academic labours of the first period and the conceptual inventiveness of the second, of a certain repetitiveness or even mannerism about the work from this time on. Baudrillard himself in his diaries even acknowledges a decline in his powers. And yet, as with all great thinkers, he is able to make something of this loss, discover in it a source of special insight and strength. For in these later writings an argument is being made not so much through their content as through their *form*. Again, Nietzsche might be the model; this time, however, not the aggressive iconoclast of the second period but the thinker of fragmented aphorisms and cultural pessimism. Baudrillard also aligns himself with the whole tradition of melancholic and disaffected essayists that runs throughout the nineteenth and twentieth centuries: Charles Baudelaire, Walter Benjamin, Theodor Adorno, Elias Canetti . . . We find in these later pieces a profound meditation upon language, its ability to operate not so much in terms of logic or persuasion but as a brief 'coming together' of words somehow to 'catch' the world and form an abstract, non-literal equivalent to it. It is perhaps this he is trying to achieve in these discursive and overlapping writings, which come so close to a kind of poetry. And poetry remains one of Baudrillard's abiding formal influences. He publishes a collection of poems as *The Stucco Angel* in 1978, and often intersperses lines of verse throughout his recent prose. It is an interest that goes all the way back, as we have seen, to his consideration of Saussure's study of anagrams in classical Roman poetry in *Symbolic Exchange and Death*. Baudrillard, in other words, is trying to find a new 'style' to fit his insights, a 'subjective' writing that understands itself as following the objective order of the world, an auto-biography without a self or even really a biography to relate . . .

It is at this point that we might return to Baudrillard under the lights of Las Vegas, leading a life after the end of things, a survivor of his own intellectual mortality. As he says at the conclusion of *Cool Memories I*: 'Everything that was pending has been finished, and whatever else comes from this point will be part of a supplementary existence, separated from the other one by this moment of lightness, of emptiness, of astonishment and relief' (*CM I*, 231). It is a life that is perhaps led as a reflection of the indifference of the world; but it is also a life – this once more the influence of Nietzsche and his fusion of free will and necessity in the doctrine of the Eternal Return – that tries to make something of this indifference, that actively strives to bring it about, that knows it does not exist without being willed. This finally is the enigma of Baudrillard's work and the difficulty of simply explaining it through the circumstances that allow it to take place. On the one hand, as with any author, we could undoubtedly set up an enormous archive of sources for and influences upon Baudrillard, showing how he is a product of the times in which he lived, the people he met, the books he read. Our summary here is a bit desultory, but a great many more details could be provided, the context in which he lived and operated made richer.[2] Ultimately, we might entirely explain Baudrillard's work, reveal how it is derivative, merely the effect of some more original cause. And yet, on the other hand, this is in the end to say nothing about it, to give no sense of its unity and power. For the characteristic of all significant thought – and Baudrillard himself speaks of this – is that, in repeating the influences upon it, it makes something else of them. The miracle of writing is that, although it is completely of this world, a reflection of it, it ends up destining or determining the world, making of it a reflection of its writing. (We are only interested in the events of an author's life insofar as they seem to be relevant to his or her writing.) As Baudrillard says: 'Writing ends up preceding life, determining it. And life ends up conforming to a sign which was initially quite cavalier. This is no doubt why so many are afraid to write' (*CM I*, 202).

This is more generally true of any attempt to explain Baudrillard's work. Although we can seek to understand it in terms of his life, his intellectual influences, even as an internal process of gradual development and refinement, there is always something about it that escapes this. For Baudrillard – this is the position he reaches at the end of his work – writing, if it is good, comes out of nothing, produces its own reality. It is 'fatal', the mere saying of it makes it true (*EC*, 101). To put this another way, it is not that these external circumstances are invalid or do not explain the writing, but that they exist only because of this writing. It is not that other authors cannot be compared to Baudrillard's work, but that we could see the Baudrillardian aspect to them only after Baudrillard himself wrote. Baudrillard's writing is neither unrelated to the world nor unexplained by it, but *doubles* it. The world just as it is – and Baudrillard's life within it – can only be understood because of it, a writing that nothing can explain. As Baudrillard expresses it in an aphorism from *Cool Memories II*:

> It is said that the chances of a monkey typing *Hamlet* are
> infinitesimal. But this is not only false, it is also misguided.
> And worse than misguided because, even if there were only
> one chance in a million that a monkey could do this, it would
> show that *Hamlet* was merely one possibility amongst many,
> which is absurd. It is the dream of weak statisticians to
> calculate the chances of producing a *Hamlet*. It is unthinkable:
> *Hamlet* does not belong to the field of possibility. It is at the
> same time radically unlikely and of the highest necessity.
> Infinitesimal probability but maximal necessity. (*CM II*, 78–9)

It is perhaps this that happens in Las Vegas that night with
Baudrillard on stage. Baudrillard precisely challenges chance
with a higher necessity, making of this chance a kind of fate or
destiny: that above the hubbub and clattering of slot machines,
through the thick French accent, something might be heard,
some brief conjuration of signs which leaves everything
untouched but after which nothing is the same, which wins
the game and breaks the bank.

* * *

There already exist a number of books on Baudrillard. The
question must be asked: why another? The easiest way we have
of saying what we are trying to do here is to say what we are
not, how we differ from what comes before. In the first full-
length book devoted to Baudrillard, *Jean Baudrillard: From
Marxism to Postmodernism and Beyond* (1989), Douglas
Kellner looks at Baudrillard's work from within a broadly
Marxist problematic. He wants to assess how adequate it is as
an account of contemporary social reality, how well it engages
in existing political conflicts, how it might serve as a guide to
future liberatory struggles. He asks: 'Does [Baudrillard] offer
illuminating insights into the deficiencies and limitations of the
targets of his provocations? Is his own position any more
convincing or useful than those he rejects?' (Kellner 1989: 123).
And he concludes:

> Radical social theory also requires empirical research into
> conditions, tendencies and developments of the present age,
> and here too Baudrillard's work is deficient, becoming ever

> more sketchy and incomplete. If he had engaged in more
> patient description of the media and popular culture, cyber-
> netics, architecture and social planning, design and semiosis,
> he could have developed a more powerful theory of social
> and cultural hegemony in the present age (although this
> would have to be supplemented by accounts of opposition,
> conflict and emancipation if it were to be genuinely pro-
> gressive and useful for radical theory and politics today).
> (1989: 213)

The next book to be written on Baudrillard is Mike Gane's
Baudrillard: Critical and Fatal Theory (1991a). Gane's approach
differs from Kellner's in two respects. First, there is a greater
interest in and approval of Baudrillard's more recent work, a
shift of emphasis away from Baudrillard as Marxist towards
Baudrillard as critic (or not) of postmodernism (1991a: 47–57).
Second, alongside this, there is a widening of his context to include
not just his early sources in Marxism but his immediate
predecessors and colleagues in French intellectual life (Jean-
Paul Sartre, Louis Althusser, Claude Lévi-Strauss, Guy Debord,
Roland Barthes, Georges Bataille, Jacques Derrida, Michel
Foucault, Julia Kristeva and Henri Lefebvre). This is continued
in Gane's follow-up volume, *Baudrillard's Bestiary: Baudrillard
and Culture* (1991b), in which a series of specific comparisons is
drawn with other thinkers over particular issues (with Marshall
McLuhan over the role of the media, with Fredric Jameson over
their respective readings of the Pompidou Centre in Paris and the
Bonaventure Hotel in Los Angeles).

Two other books on Baudrillard appear after Kellner's and
Gane's. The first, *Baudrillard and Signs: Signification Ablaze*
(1994), is by Gary Genosko. It marshals an impressive array of
semiological theories to try to sketch what it sees as the
innovation of Baudrillard's 'cancelling of the bar' between
signifier and signified in his concept of 'symbolic exchange'
(1994: xxi). The works of the linguists Roman Jakobson, Émile
Benveniste, Louis Hjelmslev and Ferdinand de Saussure are
successively taken up before Genosko turns to the American
semiotician Charles Sanders Peirce to describe best what
Baudrillard is doing. Genosko favours Peirce because he
'believes in the existence of referents' (1994: xix), something

with which he says Baudrillard would agree. The last book we
know of to have been published on Baudrillard is Charles Levin's
Jean Baudrillard: A Study in Cultural Metaphysics (1996). As
its title indicates, it attempts to elaborate a notion of 'cultural
metaphysics' with regard to Baudrillard's work, by which Levin
means to emphasize its game-like, 'negative' qualities, its fundamental rejection of meaning and sense. As he writes, citing the
Italian thinker Gianni Vattimo: 'Through a kind of philosophical
piggybacking on the nihilistic "reduction of Being to exchange-
value", cultural metaphysics is able to heighten (or to debase?)
the rational, cumulative, proto-scientific efforts of history and
social science to the level of pure speculation, denuded of all
pretence at referentiality and practicality' (1996: 7). More than
with other theoretical figures, Levin aligns Baudrillard's work
with a series of artistic movements and writers (Surrealism,
Dada, Alfred Jarry, Georges Bataille, Victor Segalen and Jorge
Luis Borges).

The first thing to be emphasized here is that we are not
simply critical of these commentators or entirely different from
them. We have already cited them in the notes to what we have
said so far, and we will be returning to them throughout what
follows. However, if we have anything to add to them here, it is
an insistence upon reading Baudrillard first of all *in his own
terms*. What does this mean? Take, for instance, Kellner's book
*Jean Baudrillard: From Marxism to Postmodernism and
Beyond*. As we suggest, it is an investigation of Baudrillard
from a Marxist point of view, an examination whose conclusion
is negative: 'This is what I believe Baudrillard's project comes
down to ultimately: capitulation to the hegemony of the Right
and a secret complicity with aristocratic conservatism' (1989:
215). But it could equally well be argued that Kellner's
approach is inappropriate from the very beginning, that it
applies Marxist criteria to a work that explicitly rejects these
(as Kellner himself notes, Baudrillard refuses Marxism and
conventional politics and moves towards a position that would
be beyond the distinction between Left and Right).[3] In a sense,
then, to evaluate Baudrillard in Marxist terms is merely to beg
the question, already to predetermine the answer the analyst

will arrive at: that Baudrillard's work is inadequate. We see a similar begging of the question with regard to Gane's *Baudrillard: Critical and Fatal Theory*. On the one hand, Gane wants to argue, as we do, that Baudrillard's work differs from normal models of criticism in that it sets the very standards by which it can be judged: 'The challenge is to follow through the logic of Baudrillard's position wherever it may lead, in the belief that this logic itself contains its own principle' (1991a: 7–8). And yet, on the other hand, there is an insistence upon comparing Baudrillard's work to that of other thinkers throughout, as though they do share the same real or set of problems, as though they were speaking of the same object.[4] We do not ourselves entirely rule out the possibility of comparing Baudrillard's work to that of other thinkers. We do so here on occasion, and – as Gane's work attests – it is necessary for pedagogical purposes, if for no other. It is just that at the same time the following questions should also be addressed, which they are not by Gane: how is it, if the respective projects of each great thinker are incommensurate, that they can be compared? What is the basis of this comparison, what do they have in common, if each creates its own reality, the terms by which it is to be assessed? What is lost in such a reading, even if valid? What is it that the very idea of comparison cannot see about the work?

Genosko's book heralds a new approach, and, we would say, with its specific emphasis upon the sign in Baudrillard, heads in the right direction. However, as Genosko himself acknowledges, it is only preliminary to such a study of the sign actually in Baudrillard's work; and, indeed, in a way the whole complex apparatus of linguistics and semiotics he brings to bear on the problem might be unnecessary. We would say – and we hope to demonstrate – that there is but one simple paradox of the sign repeated throughout all of Baudrillard's work. It is that, insofar as the copy completely resembles the original, it is no longer a copy but another original; or, to invert this, that the copy is only able to resemble the original insofar as it is different from it.[5] Genosko finally spends too much time elaborating the various theories he introduces to determine which is the best to read Baudrillard's work in sufficient detail, to show how his – or any other – concept of the sign is consistently raised and applied there. Something like this is also our objection to Levin's book, although again we find his notion of 'cultural metaphysics' very suggestive, particularly with respect to Baudrillard's later work and the importance it places on the determinate role of criticism, its power to make reality. But despite also wanting to bring out the essentially non-system-atizable nature of Baudrillard's insights, we would say that Levin's reading is not in the end systematic enough, does not pay enough attention to the inner logic and movement of Baudrillard's text. For example, it is not enough simply to say with Levin that it is 'denuded of all pretence at referentiality and practicality'. Rather, it is only through reading Baudrillard closely, slowing down and stopping the relevant stages of his argument, that we might show exactly how he avoids referentiality and practicality, or, more precisely, how these concepts are re-invented and re-inscribed in his work. Once again, for all the emphasis Levin places on the idea of language having its own power in Baudrillard, not enough weight is given to the *form* of his writing, how its meaning is to be found just as much in *how* it says something as in what it says.

To read Baudrillard in his own terms, then, what might this mean? It is to begin to think the difficulty of assessing Baudrillard in terms of some pre-existing real (as Kellner does) or applying him to new examples (as Levin does in speaking of Canada as an example of the 'fatal' object). It is to think the issues involved in comparing his work to that of other thinkers (as Gane does), or, more specifically, how his notion of the sign might compare to that of others (as Genosko does). It is to suggest that, before doing this, we must try to grasp the internal logic of Baudrillard's work, what it is already saying about its relationship to the external world, the possibility of applying theory to examples, its affinity to that of other think-ers, how the sign works and whether it can even be rep-resented. It is not definitively to stop the possibility of such things, but it is to think how it is a problem – a problem that Baudrillard himself might be addressing. It is to admit that there is a dilemma in approaching his work, that a complete and impartial understanding of it cannot be taken for granted. For, before all else, it imposes a *choice*, a choice which implies a certain decision and risk. On the one hand, we can take an *external* perspective onto Baudrillard's work, as his commentators have largely done so far, and risk merely begging the question about it, criticizing it in terms that it would not recognize or that it would reject in advance. On the other hand, we can take an *internal* perspective onto it, reading it only in its own terms, completing it as it were and risking giving it a wholeness and coherence it might not have had before us.

It is perhaps the latter risk we run here. In adopting an internal reading of Baudrillard, we open up the possibility that we are merely following him, have nothing to say about him, achieve no critical distance from him. To this we would reply that it is only within such a reading that we can be sure we are not simply begging the question of Baudrillard, proposing objections to his work that do not apply. Indeed, it is only from this internal point of view that we can even raise the methodological question of how we should approach Baudrillard, of the choice involved between internal and external readings, which is one of Baudrillard's principal concerns, although it is barely raised at all in the existing commentaries on him. (It is an issue that cannot be avoided, for even if we do not choose, even if we are not aware of the choice, we have already chosen, we have already offered an interpretation of Baudrillard.[6]) And, in fact, we would say that it is not true that no criticism of Baudrillard is possible from this internal perspective. On the contrary, we would contend that it is only from this vantage point that we can raise real objections to his work – as both the direct critics and defenders of his work cannot – pose meaningful questions as to its outside or limits. It is only by following his logic to its furthest point, by seeing it in a way as perfect, not as it *is* but as it *will be*, that we are able to discern its true ends, what it cannot speak of. It is only through reading him in his own terms that we are able to reveal the real flaws in Baudrillard's argument, which this time are not merely contingent but necessary, part of the work itself. It is only by running the risk that we repeat him that we are finally able to differ from him.

Is this not true of Baudrillard's own approach to the objects of his criticism as well? Do we not see there a series of *internal* readings of those systems he contests, criticizing them not against some external standard but by taking their own logic and pushing it to extremes (*BL*, 81–2)? That is, if we look at the various systems Baudrillard analyses throughout his career – the organization of domestic objects in *The System of Objects*, consumer society in *Consumer Society*, Marxism in *The Mirror of Production*, simulation in *Simulacra and Simulation*, the social in *In the Shadow* and the work of Foucault in 'Forget Foucault' – we discover that Baudrillard is not simply comparing them to some outside real which they exclude, but implicitly agreeing with them that there is no outside, that the real can henceforth only be defined in their terms. The problem these systems set for their interpreter is that, after them, there is no other measure by which they can be judged; it is only by applying their own criteria that they can be assessed. But Baudrillard's argument is that, even in their own terms, they fail, cannot be completed, are unable finally to explain themselves. There is always a kind of internal limit – that paradox of the sign we spoke of before – which means that, if the system is able to expand forever and nothing is outside of it, it is also never entirely closed, something is always left out of it. And it is this internal limit, this difference that makes resemblance possible, that Baudrillard calls the *real*. There are thus two different senses in which the real is used in Baudrillard's work: there is that real which is brought about by the system and that real which is the absolute limit to the system. Baudrillard's work, therefore, is not simply to be understood as the celebration of simulation, the end of the real, as so many of his commentators would have it. Rather, his problem is how to think the real when all is simulation, how to use the real against the attempts by various systems of rationality to account for it.[7] In a surprising twist, then, Baudrillard emerges as a *defender* of the real against all efforts to speak of it – including, of course, his own. As he says in his interview with Lotringer:

> But I hold no position on reality. Reality remains an unshake-
> able postulate towards which you can maintain a relation
> either of adversity or of reconciliation. The real – all things
> considered, perhaps it exists – no, it doesn't exist – is the
> insurmountable limit of theory. The real is not an objective
> state of things; it is the point at which theory can do nothing.
> This does not necessarily make of theory a failure. The real is
> actually a challenge to the theoretical edifice. But in my
> opinion theory can have no status other than that of chal-
> lenging the real. (*BL*, 122–3)

To return, finally, to those other readings of Baudrillard, we
would say they are not entirely wrong in speaking of Baudrillard in terms of the real, comparing his work to that of other
thinkers as though they were discussing the same real. But it is
the notion of the real they have in common that must be
reconceptualized. As we suggest, if we can speak of Baudrillard
in terms of a real, it is not some external real, a real that exists
out there before he comes to write of it. Instead, it is a real that
arises *within* his work, that can be seen only through its slips
and lapses, its inability to become totally self-consistent. It is
here that we find the limits to Baudrillard's own system, and it
is for just this reason that it is so important to read it closely
and in detail. This is why it is not so interesting merely to apply
Baudrillard's work to new examples or at least why this again
needs to be rethought. These examples can only be seen in
Baudrillard's terms; they exist not outside but already inside
Baudrillard's system, could only be perceived from the beginning because of it. It is a matter neither of confirming nor
denying Baudrillard's work with examples, but of thinking the
very conformity of the world to his theory and what is excluded
by it. This is also why, to conclude here, if we are to compare
Baudrillard's work to that of other thinkers, it cannot be in
terms of some external real which they all share, for each
system creates its own real, makes the world over in its image.
Rather, if there is a real they share, it might be this mutual
inability to close upon themselves, definitively to account for
themselves. If we can put it like this, it is not the same real they
share but the same *problem* of the real, the real as a problem. It
would certainly be very useful to compare Baudrillard to those

other post-structuralists to whom he is often thought in relation – and at times we do this – but this would be not so much in terms of some unambiguous real they divide between them as their common understanding of the real as the limit to all systematicity, both to those systems they analyse and to their own efforts to analyse this.

* * *

This book is divided into three chapters, each of which takes up an aspect of what we have said so far. In our first chapter, we ask what Baudrillard means by *simulation*, the attempt by the systems he analyses to represent reality. In our second chapter, we think the limits to simulation, what makes it at once possible and impossible, which Baudrillard calls *seduction*. In our third chapter, we look at language and thought as themselves this limit, at their power to affect and create the real, which Baudrillard calls the fatal and we call *doubling*. These three chapters correspond broadly to the three periods we spoke of before with regard to Baudrillard's work: the first in which he takes up the limits to scientificity and system-aticity; the second in which he considers the consequences of these for his own work; and the third in which he meditates upon how criticism and theory work. Throughout this book, therefore, we tend to look at Baudrillard's thinking on each issue in its original order of publication, trying to bring out its gradual development or elaboration, the circumstances of and even influences upon his writing. But at the same time, as we suggested earlier, we also want to gesture towards what in Baudrillard's work is not amenable to such a schema, what does not operate through the slow accumulation of evidence or data, what does not attempt to persuade or reason with the reader. On the contrary – this is what we will be addressing in our third chapter – for Baudrillard, language and thought work through short-circuiting insight, instantaneous prescription, sudden ellipsis. Baudrillard's concepts, like those systems he analyses, are not empirical descriptions of the world which can be objectively evaluated, but a kind of undemonstrable yet

irrefutable *doubling* of the way things are. After them, everything is the same but reversed, the world just as it is can only
be explained for a completely different reason. The real they
speak of and want to reveal cannot be directly pointed to, but
only alluded to metaphorically, through its very failure to be
realized. If in one way, that is, as we try to show in our first and
second chapters, Baudrillard is wanting to think the limits to
his ability to speak of the real, and thus still distance himself
from it, in another way he cannot. He is already caught up in it,
must attempt to say what it is, make the same mistakes he
cautions against – and this, strangely enough, *is* the very real
he is speaking of. He does not so much represent the real as
embody it, bring it about himself. And this again is what we
might mean by the 'fatal' or 'doubling', the saying of something
that makes it true.

To end here, this applies to us too. As with all commentaries,
we seek to master Baudrillard in these pages, criticize him as
though we could say where he goes wrong. At the same time,
however, if we do manage to capture anything of him, convey
something of the power of his thought here, it will be because
we somehow form a connection with him that goes beyond our
ability to predetermine. It will only be in losing control of our
own text, in making the same kinds of 'errors' as Baudrillard
himself. We speak of a certain paradox of the sign here as what
Baudrillard means by the real, a real that Baudrillard cannot
entirely rationalize insofar as he himself is subject to it. But we
ourselves would also be subject to this same real. This is the
final twist to Baudrillard's work and to our own project here:
it is only through the attempt to be systematic that we can
show what cannot be systematized, just as with the systems
Baudrillard analyses it is only through understanding them as
completely representing the world that he can show what they
cannot represent. We return to this in the Conclusion to our
book, where we seek to evaluate what is good and what is bad
about Baudrillard's work. This can be done, but there is also a
certain limit to any attempt to do so. We can either read it in
other terms, applying criteria to it that it would reject in
advance, thus already understanding it as failing; or we can

read it in its own terms, in which its failure is a form of success, is to bring about the very real it speaks of. This is the problematical task of any 'Introduction' to Baudrillard like this one, the very thing it should be trying to make clear insofar as it is to convey anything of his work: the impossibility of introducing Baudrillard. For it cannot be a matter of introducing Baudrillard if by that we mean a gradual, incremental acquaintanceship with his arguments and key concepts. Rather, we would say that we can never be introduced to Baudrillard, can never see him as he truly is, and have already been introduced to or perhaps seduced by Baudrillard, are already thinking in the ways he has given us or the ways he accounts for. To return to that scene we began with, we would say that to read Baudrillard is to be involved in a game with one simple rule: double your bets or fold, double or nothing (*CM I*, 81).

Notes

1. For exceptions, see Julian Pefanis, *Heterology and the Postmodern: Bataille, Baudrillard and Lyotard* (1991), and Charles Levin, *Jean Baudrillard: A Study in Cultural Metaphysics* (1996).

2. Good accounts of Baudrillard's life and the context within which he works are to be found in the Introduction to Gary Genosko, *Baudrillard and Signs: Signification Ablaze* (1994), and the Introduction and interview 'I Don't Belong to the Club, to the Seraglio', in *Baudrillard Live*.

3. Kellner admits at several points that Baudrillard would contest the standards he uses to evaluate him (1989: 124, 215).

4. Gane too raises the problem of how to read Baudrillard, but his approach is fundamentally unaffected by whatever doubts he might have (1991a: 13, 68, 209).

5. This paradox was first raised by Plato in his dialogue *Cratylus* (1875: 257), and has been treated by Derrida in his essay 'Plato's Pharmacy' (1981: 139). It is first of all in terms of this paradox that we would compare Baudrillard and Derrida and not in terms of any shared 'themes' or 'influences'.

6. Gane sees the issue of question-begging, but does not see the problem of *choice* (1991: 9–11). Levin sees this problem of choice, but does not see that it is a *forced* choice, that even not to choose is to choose (1996: 7–9).

7. It would be very interesting to make an analogy between the real we are trying to speak of here and the Lacanian 'Real'. The Lacanian Real, similarly, can only be seen through simulation, but is also a kind of hole *within*

simulation, what is left over after it. This is the point made by the Lacanian social critic Slavoj Žižek:

> What we experience as 'reality' is constituted by such a reversal: as Lacan puts it, 'reality' is always framed by a fantasy, that is, for something real to be experienced as part of 'reality', it must fit the pre-ordained co-ordinates of our fantasy-space (a sexual act must fit the co-ordinates of our imagined fantasy-scripts, a brain must fit the functioning of a computer, etc.). This way, we can propose a second definition of the Real: a surplus, a hard kernel, which resists any process of modelling, simulation or metaphorization. (1993: 43–4)

1

Simulation

In this chapter, we look at the first of the terms we have selected: simulation. Simulation is undoubtedly the word most closely associated with Baudrillard, although it is rarely understood in the sense he himself intends it. When Baudrillard's commentators speak of simulation, they often mean simply a form of illusion, the replacement of the world by its image, so that we do not experience things originally but only as a copy of something else. It is to make of Baudrillard's work a description of the 'take-over' of reality by the sign, like some science-fiction scenario. (This is the way the Australian expatriate art critic Robert Hughes understands Baudrillard in a review of *America* for *The New York Review of Books* [1992: 378–80].) Or, in an even more extreme version, simulation is seen as a form of philosophical idealism, in which the 'reality' of everyday events is completely denied. (This is the way the British deconstructionist Christopher Norris understands Baudrillard in his dispute with him over the Gulf War [1992: 14–15].[1]) In fact, what must be grasped first of all about simulation is that it is not only the loss of reality, but also its very possibility. The aim of simulation is not to do away with reality, but on the contrary to realize it, make it real. Simulation in this sense is not a form of illusion, but opposed to illusion, a way of getting rid of the fundamental illusionality of the world. This is a point Baudrillard makes clear in an interview:

> If you start from the idea that the world is a total illusion, then life, thought, become absolutely unbearable. So you have to make every effort to materialize the world, realize it, in order to escape from this total illusion. And the 'realizing' of the world, through science and technology, is precisely what simulation is – the exorcism of the terror of illusion by the most sophisticated means of the 'realization of the world'. (*BL*, 184)

The other thing to be understood about simulation, the other mistake often made with regard to it, is that it is not an empirical phenomenon, something that actually happens. Baudrillard is very well aware of the paradox that, insofar as the simulation he is describing exists, it makes any way of verifying it impossible. It means that the very real which we say is lost in simulation and against which we compare it is now only conceivable in simulated form. Indeed, we might even say that, insofar as we can speak of simulation at all, it has not yet occurred, that simulation is proved in its absence. Simulation is not real, then, but a kind of hypothesis. As Baudrillard says:

> To assert that 'we're in a state of simulation' becomes meaningless, because at that point one enters a death-like state. The moment you believe that you're in a state of simulation, you're no longer there. The misunderstanding here is the conversion of a theory like mine into a reference whereas there should never be any references. (*BL*, 166; see also *CM I*, 227)

This is why it can also be argued, against Lyotard and others, that Baudrillard is not merely nostalgic.[2] He is not simply appealing to a real that might once have been. On the contrary, the problem he sets himself is how to speak against this simulation when there is nothing to which to compare it, when there is nothing outside of it or when that outside can only be imagined in its terms. It is this question of the position of the analyst that, as we will see, is at stake in Baudrillard's account of simulation and that distinguishes it from any 'realist' understanding of it.

Indeed, what is crucial to realize about simulation is that it is not finally distinguishable from that second term we will be looking at here, seduction, and in a way is only another version of it (as seduction is only another version of simulation). The two are respective sides of the same phenomenon. What is this phenomenon? It is that paradox of representation we spoke of in our Introduction where, if the copy comes too close to the original, it no longer resembles it but is another original. There is thus an absolute limit to how close a copy can come to the original while still resembling it, or the copy only resembles the original insofar as it is different from it. And it is this limit that simulation is subject to. Simulation attempts to resemble the real, to 'realize' it, to bring out what is only implicit in it and make it explicit. But at a certain point in its progress it draws too close to the original, and further increases in perfection, instead of bringing the system closer to this original, only drive it further away. The system begins to reverse upon itself, gives rise to the opposite effects from those intended. It is this reversibility, this difference between the original and the copy, that we call seduction. But seduction, therefore, as this difference between the original and the copy, is at once what imposes a limit upon simulation and causes it to come into being. This is why seduction is not opposed to simulation but is rather its *limit* – a limit that makes it both possible and impossible.

These are the three aspects of simulation we emphasize here, which are so important to grasp and so easily misunderstood. First, it is not a simple derealization of the world but also its realization. Second, it is not a real phenomenon but only a hypothetical one, not a description of how things actually *are* but of how they *could be*. Third, it is not strictly separable from its opposite, seduction, but another side of the same process. This is why, as we will see, Baudrillard is able to argue that simulation can sometimes become a form of seduction while seduction is always in danger of becoming a form of simulation. And in all of this there is raised the difficulty of speaking of simulation, a difficulty that Baudrillard slowly realizes as his work progresses. Simulation is difficult to talk about not simply because it is not real but more profoundly because it is a total process, there is nothing outside of it. The analyst of simulation, therefore, is subject to the very rule he or she analyses. If the fundamental law of simulation is that we cannot come too close to the object represented, this is also true of the analyst's attempts to represent simulation itself. The question is thus raised, if there is nothing outside of simulation and nothing before it, how are we to think it at all? In the name of what does the analyst speak when he or she criticizes simulation, when he or she says something is excluded by it? These are the questions at stake in Baudrillard's conception of simulation.

The System of Objects

We might begin here with Baudrillard's first book, *The System of Objects*. As we said in our Introduction, amongst its various influences perhaps the two most important are the sociologist Henri Lefebvre (Baudrillard's teacher at the time) and the semiotician Roland Barthes (with whom Baudrillard was later to collaborate and teach). Indeed, Levin in his account goes further and notes that the book is an attempt to fuse the 'anti-abstraction' of Lefebvre and the 'abstraction' of Barthes (1996: 69). What does he mean by this? Lefebvre in his *Critique of Everyday Life* could be said to be the first to turn sociology's attention to the ordinary, domestic world, to the objects we surround ourselves with all the time but do not notice. It was important for Lefebvre to analyse these things exactly because their ideological effects were so easy to overlook, take for granted. His argument was that in modern consumer society we were witnessing the progressive abstraction of commodities from any real human context, that our needs and desires were increasingly subject to manipulation by outside forces. For Lefebvre, the aim of his 'critique' of everyday life was to restore an authentic relationship between people and objects, to make objects more responsive to actual needs. For Barthes, on the other hand, it was precisely a matter of breaking with Lefebvre's Marxist and phenomenological approach and its belief in a true value and meaning to objects (and, therefore, in the possibility of unalienated needs and desires with regard to them). In a series of famous analyses in his book *Mythologies*, he showed how our relationships with objects were not direct but always mediated by the sign. Objects, that is, are taken up not in terms of their use or function but primarily to communicate. Objects form a kind of language, within which such values as use and function become merely rhetorical. There is not some underlying denotation to the object, but only an endless succession of connotations.

Baudrillard inherits these two contrasting approaches of Lefebvre and Barthes towards the everyday object. Indeed, the implicit tension between them is even greater in Baudrillard's book because he will generalize Barthes's argument, forcing his conclusions to their furthest reach. Barthes's *Mythologies* remains a series of studies of single objects. To this extent, it remains phenomenological in approach. It is as though the individual object can still be focused upon, exists in itself. For Baudrillard, however, one of the consequences of the object's entry into the field of the sign is that, just like the individual elements of a language, no object has any meaning in itself but only in its relationship with other objects. In a sense, that is, it is the very system of objects which precedes the possibility of any single object, the series which produces the uniqueness of any particular model. And, similarly, we as consumers do not so much directly desire any specific object as desire only in a competitive relationship with others (as mediated by such things as status and prestige). We desire only another's desire. Baudrillard in this regard emphasizes much more than Barthes the inherent abstraction of the system of objects, so much so that we must ask what is the status of those dazzling examples he provides throughout his book, for this is to remain after all on the level of description, to make us think that the system of objects can be grasped through its constituent parts. And yet at the same time Baudrillard also wants to speak, like Lefebvre, against the system of objects, to name what it excludes or, indeed, to show in the end why there is no such thing as a system of objects, why any 'description of the system of objects cannot be divorced from a critique of that system's practical ideology' (*SO*, 10).

This, finally, is the paradoxical task of *The System of Objects*. With Barthes, Baudrillard wants to reveal that function and use are no longer real but only effects of the sign, no longer active forces underpinning the system of objects but only rhetorical values within it (and that they were perhaps like this from the very beginning). With Lefebvre, Baudrillard wants to talk of what is excluded from this system of objects, what the limit is to its organization through signs. But we might analyse in more detail here this ambiguity of the system of objects in both expressing and doing away with use-value and need, for it is this ambiguity which is to run throughout the rest of Baudrillard's work and which constitutes the problem of simulation.

The System of Objects is divided up into four sections. The first three are devoted to the object in its various registers – functional or objective; non-functional or subjective; meta- or dysfunctional – and the fourth to what Baudrillard calls the 'socio-ideological' system of objects and their consumption. The first, we might say, takes up the object within the frame-work of use; the second as antique or as belonging to a collection; the third as gadget or novelty. The fourth looks at how the system produces the desire for these objects via advertising and credit. We deal with the first section here, but we will see that in a way the second register, that of the non-functional or subjective object, is not really so different. What we find is that, if the functional or objective can always become non-functional or subjective, so too can the non-functional or subjective become functional or objective. Indeed – and this explains Baudrillard's third section – all objects ultimately become both meta- and dysfunctional. Before all else, they speak of their own functioning (are meta-functional) and thus become non-functional (dysfunctional). In the end, all objects become gadgets: signifiers of usefulness, in fact hyper-, multi-functional, but for all that useless. All this within a system in which consumption and desire need to be produced, as the fourth section demonstrates, because objects themselves are no longer good for anything, no longer function as objects.

The first section of *The System of Objects*, consistent with Baudrillard's ambition to analyse objects in terms of the sign, divides the objective order of objects up into two categories. The first is objects in terms of their *arrangement*, the successive disposition or organization of objects in time and space, which we might analogize to the *syntagmatic* order of language. The second is objects in terms of their *atmosphere*, the mutually exclusive decisions as to what colour or material to make an object out of, which we might analogize to the *paradigmatic* order of language. In terms of arrangement, Baudrillard looks at the shift from the interiorized, centred organization of furniture within the old bourgeois interior, in which domestic space is enclosed, cut off from the outside, and objects are heavy, immobile and often reflective (mirrors, the polished surfaces of tables, grandfather clocks), to our current open, modular, outward-facing living environments, in which furniture is no longer fixed in space or function but able to be broken down and re-assembled in various combinations: 'Beds become couches, and sideboards and wardrobes give way to built-in storage' (*SO*, 17). As opposed to the isolation and individuality of the furniture in bourgeois interiors – a mark of their ethic of self-reliance and independence, or at least of the centrality of the family – furniture in this new environment is now only able to be grasped in its relationship with its surroundings. No piece of furniture and no space in the house stands alone: 'The substance and form of the old furniture have been abandoned for good, in favour of an extremely free game of functions' (*SO*, 21). The old order was psychological, unconscious, interior and subjective. The new arrangement is functional, conscious, exterior and objective. The inhabitants – or, better, consumers – of this new space become just as much analysts of arrangement as the sociologists who study them. They are all '*hommes de rangement*' or 'interior designers' (*SO*, 26).

Baudrillard takes up the same shift in terms of atmosphere, the paradigmatic relationship between objects. The same increasing abstraction can be seen, for instance, in the colours in which these new domestic interiors are painted. Once, colour was understood as a reflection of the world outside, with no other justification needed than this equivalence. Then, colour only symbolically or metaphorically gestured towards this outside. It was as an *analogy* to something else that it was painted, an analogy which necessitated its comparison with other colours. Finally, all links to the outside are broken and colour is *only* understood in terms of its relationship to other colours, a relationship which necessitates its comparison with *every other* colour. No colour can henceforth be grasped on its own but only on the basis of its comparison with others. A 'hot' colour, for example, is not hot in itself but only because of its difference from cold colours, just as a 'cold' colour is cold only because it is not hot: '"Functional" warmth is thus a warmth that no longer issues forth from a warm substance, or from a harmonious juxtaposition of particular objects, but instead arises from the systematic oscillation or abstract synchrony of a perpetual "warm-and-cold" which in reality continually defers any "warm" feeling' (*SO*, 37). Thus the rise of pastels (*SO*, 32–3) for Baudrillard, which are not so much a particular colour as the mixture of all colours, colours that can be combined with every other colour because they virtually contain all of them.

There is also a similar cutting free of substance from any prior reality, whether natural or symbolic, to be seen in the choice of materials to make up any particular object. Interestingly, in terms of our previous argument about the way use and functionality become mere tactical values within the system of objects, we see the same thing with 'naturality' here. With the rise of artificial materials, for example plastic, real wood suddenly becomes a less practical option to make an object out of. We would choose wood only as part of a *moral* preference for the natural (*SO*, 38) – a natural that itself no longer comes from nature but can only be grasped as the opposite of the artificial within the order of signs. The very idea that it can be chosen at all makes nature artificial. On the other hand, to continue to cast artificial objects in natural shapes, for example plastic veneer with a grain of wood, testifies precisely to the continued appeal of the sign of the natural, its rhetorical weight within the system of objects. And it is within this regime of signs that glass becomes the privileged substance. It is not for any ostensible material advantage that we would select glass as a substance out of which to make our objects – on the contrary, glass is fragile, breakable, shows up smudges – but because of its connotations of clarity, neutrality and impartiality. The transparency and lack of interiority of glass – the decor *par excellence* of modern interiors – is a *moral* statement about freedom, accountability, the open and unimpeded exchange between different spaces and functions. At once 'close and distant, intimate and the refusal of intimacy, communicable and non-communicable', glass founds an apparent 'transparency without transmission': 'we can see, but not touch' (*SO*, 41–2). Objects made of glass, like surfaces painted in pastel, implicitly include all others, which can be seen behind them – and this is itself understood as a form of liberty and self-expression.

Finally in the field of atmosphere, Baudrillard notes the recent trend towards remote control and miniaturization in our relationship to objects. As with furniture, colour and materials, he charts a progressive diminution of the physicality of the things around us and their increasing abstraction as signs. There is at first manual labour, then mechanical manipulation, then lastly cybernetic command and virtualization. Here too this breaking away from physical reality is understood as a kind of liberation – a liberation both of objects themselves and of the humans who use them. Now, the presumed functionality of objects is unlimited, not constrained by any inability to manipulate them. Labour becomes less a matter of 'neuromuscular praxis' and more a 'cerebro-sensory vigilance' (*SO*, 49). We move into the era of the man-machine, all the way from primitive automata and robots to super-sophisticated computers and – although obviously Baudrillard does not speak of this yet – actual machines of alternate or virtual reality.

In each case here, we see something of what Baudrillard means by simulation. It is not the mere abstraction or derealization of the object, its passing over from material presence to sign, as some commentators would suggest. Rather, it is as it were the consequence of this. On the one hand, something like functionality (or naturality) is spoken of more than ever, given greater emphasis than ever before. Interior furniture is no longer fixed, immobile, determined in function and place, but variable, multi-purpose, adaptable. The colours and materials that make up the object are no longer rooted in either nature or the symbolic (cultural conventions), but are able to be freely chosen, a completely optional addition to the object. The increasing trend towards remote control and miniaturization allows the improved manipulation of and mastery over objects, a bringing of them closer to the mind and intention of the user. Even the design of ordinary items like cigarette lighters, which are now shaped like sea-rounded pebbles to fit into the hand (*SO*, 58–9), and cars, which have aerodynamic fins added to them (*SO*, 59–60), seem to reflect their implicit purpose better than ever before. The use and function of objects no longer remain unconscious, haphazard, something beyond their control, but are something rigorously aimed at by them, immanent within the order of signs by which they are constructed and programmed.

On the other hand, however, as Baudrillard also tries to make clear, if function and its attendant values naturality and culturality are expressed better than ever, we also have the feeling that they are inauthentic, unreal, merely a tactical or rhetorical value within the system of signs. We no longer have these values as such but only something that stands in for them, resembles them, uses them as an alibi. With modern furniture, there seems to be a kind of freedom guaranteed by its mobility, the interconnectedness between space and function it allows, but this is only an *image* of freedom. That immediate openness to the outside and the scrutiny of others is the very opposite of freedom, is ultimately to do away with that interiority and free will which make individual choice possible. With the colours and materials that make up the object, the simple ability to choose is understood as a form of self-expression, without realizing that we can henceforth choose one colour only to choose all the others, that all choices are in the end the same. With miniaturization and remote control, humans are said to liberate the object and the object humans, but it is only objects in the image of the human, the human in the image of the object. The human and the object are from now on inseparable, far from free but each dependent on the other. With cigarette lighters and car fins, the object is said to express nature and function better than ever, but it is a nature that is already culturalized, a function that cannot be used. They are a nature and function that are only possible on the basis that they are forbidden, nothing more than a 'pretext' which 'does no more than signify the *idea* of the function' (*SO*, 60).

This is the paradox of simulation, or rather the paradox upon which simulation founders. At the same time the system expresses function better than ever and we do not have real function but only a function on the basis of the sign. From now on, function must have the commutability or exchangeability of the sign or it is not function at all. (As with glass in the order of atmosphere, which is at once 'close and distant, intimate and the refusal of intimacy, communicable and non-communicable', everything becomes a sign of a sign, an allegory of the system itself. It is this that perhaps ultimately justifies Baudrillard's method of proceeding from examples, even though there are in fact no examples before the system.) Against this, Baudrillard is suggesting that function and use, as in the old bourgeois interiors, must be something unconscious, outside the order of signs, something that cannot be encoded. As soon as the object is consciously designed with its use in mind, this is no longer true use but only an image or simulacrum of use. As Baudrillard writes in the Conclusion to the first section of *The System of Objects*:

> The functional system is thus characterized, *in a thoroughly ambiguous way*, on the one hand by a *transcendence* of the traditional system under its three aspects – as the primary function of the object, as drives and primary needs, and as a set of symbolic relations between the two – and on the other hand by a simultaneous *disavowal* of these three mutually re-inforcing aspects of the traditional system. In other words:
>
>   1. The coherence of the functional system of objects depends on the fact that these objects – along with their various properties, such as colour, form, and so on – no

longer have any value of their own, but merely a universal value as signs. [. . .]

2. The always *transcended* presence of Nature (in a far more consistent and exhaustive fashion than in any earlier culture) is what confers on this system its validity as a cultural model and its objective dynamism. (*SO*, 63–4)

This paradox of *simulation* is to be Baudrillard's essential subject, although he does not use that word yet. It is why the highest point of the systematicity of objects corresponds to the impossibility of a system of objects, why if the system of objects is a language it ultimately has nothing to say. It is the *internal* limit to the system of objects: not the fact that use is simply not referred to or only a rhetorical value within it, but that, in being immanent to it, in becoming a function of the sign, it is also lost. But a complicated question is raised here, which Baudrillard does not yet address. For, it might be asked, if the system of objects is the most complete expression of function, if function is henceforth only imaginable in the form of the sign, how can Baudrillard actually say what is excluded from the system of objects? To what extent is he able to speak from somewhere outside of it? We might put this another way. In his analysis of the functional order of objects, Baudrillard characterizes that moment before the object's entry into the system of the sign. It is for him the bourgeois order of objects, in which use is unconscious, instinctual and psychological (*SO*, 21), in which objects are not seen in their modern-day functionalist form. And yet, from the perspective of simulation itself, this time before the system can only be seen as a variation *within* it. The bourgeois non-awareness of the rhetoric of function can only be understood as a deliberate refusal of it, as in the subjective register of objects Baudrillard will deal with in the second section of the book (where wealthy people, who have already satisfied all their needs, deliberately choose non-functional, archaic or antique objects to conjure up a by-gone era, the fact that they are not ruled by the dictates of function, in a sort of hyper-consumption [*SO*, 73–84]). This again raises the position of the analyst *vis-à-vis* his or her object of analysis, for if, as Baudrillard says, practitioners within the system of objects are also in a way critics, standing outside of it and trying to say how it works, then so too are its critics only practitioners, not outside of it but part of it, what the system already takes into account and plays on. These two difficulties – the problem of naming an outside to simulation and the position of the analyst in relation to it – are not taken up in *The System of Objects*, are not seen as a problem there, and as such are a failing of the book. But they are issues that are increasingly to come to dominate Baudrillard's work as it progresses.

'The Orders of Simulacra'

The essay 'The Orders of Simulacra', though it first appears in English with 'The Precession of Simulacra' in the volume *Simulations*, is in fact a chapter from Baudrillard's *Symbolic Exchange and Death*. In keeping with the still sociological intention of that book, the chapter is Baudrillard's attempt to write another history of simulation.[3] Indeed, as its title indicates, it is an attempt to recast and criticize Michel Foucault's famous *The Order of Things* (1977a). (This connection is only apparent in English, for the original French title of Foucault's book translates out as *Words and Things*.) In other words, just as Foucault wanted to write a history of representation there, so here Baudrillard wants to write a history of simulation – a history that will in a sense be critical of the realist pretensions of Foucault's effort. But if 'The Orders of Simulacra' is a history of simulation, it is also an analysis of its logic. In it for the first time in Baudrillard's work there is a detailed following through of the fundamental paradox of simulation that if two things resemble each other too closely they no longer resemble each other at all. Interestingly, this is not so different from Foucault's own *The Order of Things*, which also dwells on the same enigma.[4] This should not surprise us, for, as we have tried to argue, the paradox of simulation Baudrillard discovers is the same as the paradox of representation, Baudrillard's investigation of simulation is part of a much longer debate about the nature of representation.

In 'The Orders of Simulacra', Baudrillard identifies three different orders or stages of simulation (again like Foucault in *The Order of Things*, who similarly distinguishes three *epistemes* of representation). The first order he identifies is that of the counterfeit, based on what he calls the 'natural' ('OS', 83) law of value, and it runs all the way from the Renaissance up to the Industrial Revolution. In the counterfeit, the sign for the first time breaks free from the 'reciprocal obligation' ('OS', 84) between classes, castes and clans that marked feudal society, and begins to refer to some external reality. It is no longer directly exchanged from person to person but only through some common or agreed-upon third, which performs the role of the medium of exchange. Thus two signs can be compared to each other insofar as they both seem to refer to the same outside object or reality. This is why Baudrillard can call this era of the sign that of the counterfeit, but also why it is through this counterfeit that signs are true. It is because within this first order signs do not directly attempt to pass themselves off as real but only exchange themselves for each other through their shared recognition of some external real. Signs only refer to the real, we might say, through their difference from it.

Thus the typical Baroque forms of stucco and the automaton. Stucco attempts to be illusionistic, to convince the spectator it is real, but its entire aesthetic effect depends upon his or her recognition that it is not real, that it is an illusion. Like *trompe l'oeil*, another of the great aesthetic expressions of the time, the illusion at first convinces us, but a slight change of perspective alters everything. What we admire in stucco, then, is not simply its resemblance to the real but precisely its minute difference from the real. It can become the general equivalent of all other substances not because it directly resembles the world but because it marks the difference between all other substances and the world. Baudrillard writes: 'Stucco exorcizes the unlikely confusion of matter into a single new substance, a sort of general equivalent of all the others, and is prestigious theatrically because it is itself a representative substance, a mirror of all the others' ('OS', 88).

We see the same thing with the automaton. The automaton charms or moves us not because it imitates humans or is meant to be mistaken for them, but because of the uncanny difference between it and humans. The automaton is a *metaphor for* and not an *equivalent to* the human. It reveals something about us in its very difference from us. Again, as Baudrillard says:

> The automaton has no other destiny than to be ceaselessly compared to living man [. . .]. A perfect double for him, right up to the suppleness of his movements, the functioning of his organs and intelligence – right up to touching upon the anguish there would be in becoming aware that there is no difference, that the soul is over with and now it is an ideally naturalized body which absorbs its energy. The difference is then always maintained, as in the case of that perfect auto-maton that the impersonator's jerky movements on stage imitate; so that at least, even if the roles were reversed, no confusion would be possible. ('OS', 93–4)

And the objects within this first order of simulacra are some-how modest, know the limits to their aspirations to be real, that it is only in their difference from the real that their relationship to it can be maintained. This is perhaps the true order of knowledge that can be attributed to the automaton, the mind or will it can be said to possess.

The second order of simulacra is that of production, based on the 'commercial' ('OS', 83) law of value, and it corresponds to the period of the Industrial Revolution. This is only an intermediate period, says Baudrillard, 'rather inadequate as an imaginary solution to the problem of mastering the world' ('OS', 98), 'ephemeral' ('OS', 100), an 'episode' ('OS', 97) of less interest than either the first or third orders. It is a moment made possible by the initial freeing-up of signs we see in the first period of simulation, but without that total indetermination we have in the third. What we find in this second period is the gradual loss of the difference between sign and reality, copy and original, that characterized the first period and made their resemblance possible. Within this second order, sign and reality simply become equivalent. The sign does not merely allude to the real via its difference from it, but wants to be the *same as* it – and it is at this point that it no longer resembles the real at all.

The defining example of this loss of the difference between the original and copy that characterizes the Industrial Revolution is the serial reproducibility of the assembly line. The whole rationale of the assembly line, of course, is that there be no difference between the model and the series. The first version of the thing is the same as the last. All copies are, as it were, 'original'. And all are, equally, 'unoriginal'. They are certainly no longer counterfeits because there is no real or original from which they derive, against which to compare them. As Baudrillard says:

> The relation [between objects on an assembly line] is no longer that of an original to its counterfeit – neither analogy nor reflection – but equivalence, indifference. In a series, objects become undefined simulacra one of the other. And so, along with the objects, do the men that produce them. Only the obliteration of the original reference allows for the generalized law of equivalence, that is to say the *very possibility of production*. ('OS', 97)

We might also compare the robot which characterizes this second order of simulacra with that automaton which characterized the first. If it was the difference of the automaton from the human that allowed us to compare them, it is the very identicality of the robot to the human which means there is no longer any relationship between the two. The robot is no longer in any competitive rivalry with the human – that Promethean/ Frankensteinian myth disappears with the first order of simulacra – they are instead two entirely separate and parallel phenomena. The achievements of robots far outstrip those of humans and can only be understood in their own terms. As Baudrillard writes:

> The robot no longer interrogates appearance; its only truth is in its mechanical efficacy. It is no longer turned towards a resemblance with man, to whom furthermore it no longer bears comparison. That infinitesimal metaphysical difference, which made all the charm and mystery of the automaton, no longer exists; the robot has absorbed it for its own benefit. Being and appearance are melded into a

common substance of production and work. [. . .] No more
resemblance or lack of resemblance, but an immanent logic
of the operational principle. ('OS', 94–5)

The third order of simulacra is that of simulation properly
speaking, based on what Baudrillard calls the 'structural' ('OS',
83) law of value, and it runs from the Industrial Revolution up
to the present day. It continues that liberation of the sign we
see in the first and second orders, but with this difference: that
whereas there we seem to witness the progressive disappearance of the real in the self-referentiality of the sign, here we
have an attempt to speak of it again. By means of a mediated
and deliberately introduced difference within the code, the
system seeks to recapture something of the contingencies and
fluctuations of the real – a little like those small 'variations'
introduced into the system of objects to bring about a stream of
marginally differentiated objects ('OS', 101, 105). But in both
cases, it is only a *simulated* real, an *effect* of reality. It is not a
real outside of the code, as in the first order, but a real that
arises – like use and function in *The System of Objects* – only
as an excuse, an alibi, a 'tactical hallucination' ('OS', 117),
within it. That is, if the system justifies itself on the basis of
capturing some pre-existing real or expressing a prior reality,
what is realized is that this real is possible only because of the
system, only leads to a further extension of the system.

Examples of this third order of simulacra include the referenda and questionnaires that mark modern democracies and
the post-Industrial form of duopoly (as opposed to the Industrial form of monopoly). In the referendum or questionnaire, a
certain space seems to be given to the other. Like the scientist's
attempt to discover empirical reality, the pollster appears to be
allowing events to surprise him or her or upset his or her
expectations. However, if the questioner thus opens him- or
herself up to the difference of the other, the very form this
other's answer can take is dictated by his or her question. The
respondent can only reply in a manner dictated by the poll
itself, and any surprise is in a way what is predicted and
accounted for by it in advance. Question and answer are bound
together in a kind of circularity, each in a sense dependent on

the other. The system, despite opening itself up to the outside, once again merely constitutes it in its image ('OS', 131–2).

The same thing can be seen with the contemporary form of duopoly, that is, two major parties sharing power or two companies the market. If the first crude form of the Industrial Revolution was that of monopoly – too harsh, too open to sudden collapse – the post-Industrial form is that of duopoly: a model that, while seeming to open itself up to competition, in fact prohibits it more than ever. Now, even the outside to the monopolistic regime is not true competition, niche markets, etc., but only its continuation: another monopoly. All competition, otherness, is co-opted, made to work, within an expanded capitalistic schema: it is simply harder to compete against two companies than one. As Baudrillard says:

> It might appear that the historical movement of capital carries it from open competition towards oligopoly, then towards monopoly – that the democratic movement goes from multiple parties towards bipartism, then toward the single party. Nothing of the sort. Oligopoly or the current duopoly results from a *tactical doubling of monopoly*. In all domains duopoly is the final stage of monopoly. [. . .] Power is absolute only if it is capable of diffraction into various equivalents, only if it knows how to take off so as to put more on. This goes for brands of soapsuds as well as peaceful co-existence. You need two superpowers to keep the universe under control: a single empire would crumble of itself. ('OS', 133–4)

'The Precession of Simulacra'

Baudrillard further explores the consequences of this third order of simulacra – its power to produce the real – in the subsequent essay 'The Precession of Simulacra', originally published as part of the collection *Simulacra and Simulation*. It is this essay, along with 'The Orders of Simulacra', that first made Baudrillard's name, particularly in the English-speaking world. 'The Precession of Simulacra', especially, is full of dazzling twists of logic, brilliant and memorable examples. It is still perhaps the most quoted of Baudrillard's writings, understood as embodying all that is best and worst about his work. Critics are quick to point out its seeming disregard of common sense and everyday reality, followers keen to apply its arguments to other situations. But, again, as we said in our Introduction, it is important, before seeing Baudrillard as simply describing events, to read him in his own terms, to discern the fundamental logic that underpins his assertions. It is to understand first of all that the examples he uses are not literal but metaphorical, function to gesture towards something more abstract. This is not to say they have no relationship to the real, but to ask before all else what their relationship is to the real, what they say about their relationship to the real. For, as with all simulacra, they make the world over in their image. They do not simply precede their theory as what would either justify or refute it, but are the real conjured up by that theory as its 'outside' or 'other'. In a way, therefore, these examples are both examples of this logic of simulation and evidence of its limits, and it is this ambivalence we will be exploring here.

Baudrillard begins 'The Precession of Simulacra' by offering, as in *The System of Objects* and 'The Orders of Simulacra', another short history of simulation, this time based on Jorge Luis Borges's well-known fable, 'Of Exactitude in Science', about a map of an empire so detailed that it completely covers the territory it was meant to plot – a map which ends up becoming 'frayed and finally ruined, a few shreds still discernible in the deserts' ('PS', 1). But if this image of a map entirely covering its territory is startling, it is only an example for Baudrillard of the 'discreet charm of second-order simulacra' ('PS', 1), the equivalence between the simulacrum and the real. Today, says Baudrillard, the terms of this allegory need to be reversed. It is not the territory that precedes the map, but the map that precedes the territory. It is not the map that resembles the territory, but the territory that resembles the map. It is the real not the map which is disappearing and turning into desert, the 'desert of the real' ('PS', 2). But, even inverted, Baudrillard continues, the allegory is useless. For – and this is where he picks up again that paradox of representation we have been looking at – with the loss of that 'sovereign difference' ('PS', 2) between the map and the territory, it is no longer properly speaking a matter either of a map or a territory, there simply being no relationship at all between them. And it is this loss of contact between the original and the copy that leads to that artificial revival of the real we see in the third order of simulacra, its re-introduction of difference and otherness in an attempt to keep referentiality functioning, to forestall the collapse of representation. But it is an otherness that is only possible because of the system, that only leads to a further loss of the real, for if the system has lost touch with reality by a too-close proximity to the real, then adding more real to it merely takes it further away.

Baudrillard provides a beautiful example of the way this simulation appears to open itself up to the other only to do away with it towards the beginning of 'The Precession of Simulacra'. He recounts there the extraordinary day when, against the whole forward march of science, its insatiable desire to domesticate and explain the world, the anthropologists and ethnographers of the Philippines decided to return the Stone-Age Tasaday Indians to the rainforest where they had recently been discovered after having lived there undisturbed for some eight centuries. Now, it might be thought that this was an effort by science to think its proper limits, the fact that it always turns its object into a simulacrum, to save these Indians by putting them 'out of the reach of colonists, tourists and ethnologists', after seeing them 'decompose immediately upon contact like a mummy in the open air' ('PS', 13). However, insists Baudrillard, it was not in order to save the Indians that the ethnographers put them back into the forest, but to save *themselves*. Ethnography, like any other system, only exists at a certain remove from the object it analyses – and it was this distance that was disappearing with the sudden apparition of these Indians. This was the real 'decomposition' of the Indians that had to be stopped, one not so much from the diseases of civilization as into the very science that was studying them. They were becoming unreal, simulacra of themselves, precisely in becoming too real, too accessible. It was this distance, therefore, that had to be restored. These Indians had to be returned to the forest from where they came. Baudrillard comments wryly:

> At this point begins a persistent anti-ethnology to which Jaulin, Casteneda and Clastres variously belong. In any case, the logical evolution of a science is to distance itself ever further from its object until it dispenses with it entirely: its autonomy ever more fantastical in reaching its pure form. The Indian thereby driven back into the ghetto, into the glass coffin of virgin forest, becomes the simulation model for all conceivable Indians *before ethnology*. The latter thus allows itself the luxury of being incarnate beyond itself, in the 'brute' reality of these Indians it has entirely re-invented – Savages who are indebted to ethnology for still being Savages: what a triumph for this science which seemed dedicated to their destruction! ('PS', 14–15)

This is as we have seen in the third order of simulacra in 'The Orders of Simulacra': ethnology produces, simulates, an other to itself – real Indians back in the forest, anti-ethnology – but this other is only possible because of it, only leads to a further extension of it. Henceforth, after simulation – this is its real effect – we are only able to imagine this other or anterior to simulation in terms of simulation itself. And we mean this not only for those actual Tasaday Indians transported back into the forest, but for 'all conceivable Indians *before ethnology*' ('PS', 15). In other words, after the hypothesis of simulation, everything can only be conceived of as though it were simulated, even if it is not.[5] Even if we do not have the actual objects or discourses of simulation themselves – as Baudrillard emphasizes, we do not have Indians in the hand but only in the bush, do not have ethnology but only a persistent anti-ethnology – this other is only possible because of them, can only be understood in terms of them. The world as it is can only be grasped on the basis of simulation. Simulation *doubles* the world. This is why Baudrillard can say: 'We [in our very difference from, or even indifference to, the Tasaday] are all Tasaday' ('PS', 16).

Hence the wonderful, paradoxical examples of 'The Precession of Simulacra' – examples both that made the essay famous and that seem to capture so succinctly the ironies of our contemporary situation. Of Disneyland: 'Disneyland is there to conceal the fact that it is the "real" country, all of "real" America, which is Disneyland' ('PS', 25). Of Watergate: 'Watergate is not a scandal: this is what must be said at all costs, for this is what everyone is concerned to conceal' ('PS', 28). Of the Vietnam War: 'Ultimately, this war was only a crucial episode in a peaceful co-existence' ('PS', 67). And of the bombing in Hanoi during it: 'The intolerable nature of this bombing should not conceal the fact that it was only a simulacrum designed to allow the Vietnamese to seem to countenance a compromise, and Nixon to make the Americans swallow the retreat of their forces' ('PS', 69). And, finally, of nuclear armament:

> Responsibility, control, censorship, self-deterrence always increase faster than the forces or weapons at our disposal. This is the secret of the social order. [. . .] Thus it is altogether likely that one day we shall see the nuclear powers exporting atomic reactors, weapons and bombs to every latitude. After control by threat will succeed the much more effective strategy of pacification by the bomb and its possession. ('PS', 73)

These examples are provocative, scandalous, unsentimental. They are both what Baudrillard's supporters laud as his insight into modern reality and what his detractors condemn for their ignorance and disavowal of authentic human suffering and undeniable truth. Vietnam as merely an 'episode in a peaceful co-existence'? What about the 60,000 dead American soldiers and countless Vietnamese soldiers and civilians? Nuclear weapons as the impossibility of their use? What about Hiroshima and Nagasaki? And yet, as we say, before either celebrating or condemning Baudrillard, before seeing him as describing the world or seeking to apply his theories to the world, we must discern the underlying logic behind these examples, the fact that what they already raise is the nature of their relationship to the real. For what is being repeated each time here? It is the logic of the third order of simulacra, in which the system puts forward an other to itself so that it is proved all the more. The system opens itself up to the other, but it is an other that is only possible because of the system. We do not have the system as such, but the world in its very indifference and otherness can only be explained because of it.

Thus, with Disneyland, a special place of childhood is marked off to demonstrate that the rest of America is by contrast grown-up, whereas in fact it is the '"real" country, all of "real" America, which is Disneyland' ('PS', 25). With Watergate, the denunciation of the scandal testifies that, as opposed to this, there is a moral law in politics: 'And Watergate, above all, succeeded in imposing the idea that Watergate was a scandal' ('PS', 27). With the Vietnam War, there is a war only to hide the fact that a pact or accord between the two countries has been struck, in which the real enemy is neither side as such but a radical third, which must be excluded: 'The two adversaries are fundamentally as one against that other, unnamed, never mentioned thing [. . .] tribal, communal, pre-capitalist structures, every form of exchange, language and symbolic organization' ('PS', 68-9).[6] And the Americans in turn admitted defeat only to allow Vietnam and China to recognize that they had lost the real war, that of their incorporation into Western democracy or the American-run new world order: '[The Vietnam War] was only a crucial episode in a peaceful co-existence. It marked China's apprenticeship in a global *modus vivendi* [. . .] and, to this extent, the USA pulled out of Vietnam but won the war' ('PS', 67). Finally, with the nuclear bomb, the terror of an atomic explosion is only a distraction from an even greater terror and deterrence inaugurated under its name, the fact that 'lockdown and control grow as fast as (and undoubtedly even faster than) liberating possibilities' ('PS', 74). In each case, the system puts forward its other as real – Disneyland, scandal, war, the nuclear – only in order to exclude the real: the fact that all of America is child-like; that there is no morality in politics; Vietnamese agrarian societies based on symbolic exchange; the terror of nuclear deterrence. From now on, this other to the system can only be thought of in its terms, only goes to prove it all the more. The real strategy of the system in putting forward its other is ultimately to get rid of this other.

* * *

'The Precession of Simulacra' is in a sense Baudrillard's definitive statement of simulation, one which he will never go beyond. (Later, in *The Transparency of Evil*, he will speak of a so-called fourth order of simulacra, one based on a 'viral' or 'fractal' order of value, but this is in fact no different from the third [*TE*, 5].) And it is this ability of the third order of simulation to produce its own other that is to be the abiding concern throughout Baudrillard's work, for the essential problem he addresses there is how to name a limit to the systems of simulation he looks at, how to think what is outside of them or what they exclude. It is the problem of *The System of Objects*, where he tries to speak of the 'function', 'drives' and the 'symbolic relations' between them disavowed by the system of objects. It is the problem of 'The Orders of Simulacra' and 'The Precession of Simulacra', where he tries to speak of the 'real' deferred by various systems of simulation. It is the problem of *For a Critique of the Political Economy of the Sign*, where he tries to speak of the 'referent' left out by the transformation of everything into signifier (*PE*, 127–9). It is the problem of *The Mirror of Production*, where he tries to speak of that 'utopia' and poetic 'speech' excluded by Marxism in always thinking of nature and human beings in terms of production (*MP*, 163–7). But it is a problem because, insofar as Baudrillard wants to think what is excluded from these systems, he could do so only in terms of them. He could do so only to repeat the very strategy of these systems themselves in proposing an other to them by which they are proved.

There is thus a certain 'double strategy' (*SSM*, 107) necessary on the part of Baudrillard in attempting to think the outside to these systems of simulation. On the one hand, he has to name this outside, something they actually exclude. But, on the other hand, he must realize that he cannot name this outside, that any outside is only an effect of the system itself. He has to think, therefore, not so much what is outside or other to the system of simulation as what is excluded by the fact that it has no outside. He has to think what is excluded by the very conformity of the world to the system, the fact that from now on it can only be seen in its image. And it is in terms of this necessary 'double strategy', his ability to keep both of these constraints simultaneously in mind, that we would judge Baudrillard – a judgement that Baudrillard cannot avoid because it is a judgement in his own terms, in relation to the very problem he sets himself. Take, for instance, the following passage from 'The Precession of Simulacra':

> As long as it was historically threatened by the real, power risked deterrence and simulation, disintegrating every contradiction by means of the production of equivalent signs. When it is threatened today by simulation (the threat of vanishing in the play of signs), power risks the real, risks crisis; it gambles on remanufacturing artificial, social, economic, political stakes. This is a question of life or death for it. But it is too late. ('PS', 44)

Baudrillard says here that the system's attempt to remanufacture the real as in the third order of simulacra is 'too late', that its ability to do so is a symptom of the very problem it is trying to overcome. And this is true. But what Baudrillard thereby forgets is that it is precisely not 'too late': the system of simulation never actually collapses or comes to an end. For, if its increased perfection takes the system further away from the real, it also means that it is more real than ever. The system both ends and is completed as in *The System of Objects*. There is no way, therefore, of saying the system simply fails, as Baudrillard does here, except in terms of the system itself. We would rather say that it is a *limit* to the system, a limit that makes the system both possible and impossible. And it is crucial to read all of the work we have looked at so far in terms of this 'error'. The loss of functionality Baudrillard speaks of in the objective register of objects in *The System of Objects* would be no different from its deliberate rejection within the subjective register. The real Baudrillard speaks of as excluded by simulation in 'The Orders of Simulacra' and 'The Precession of Simulacra' would be no different from the third order of simulacra's own deliberate production of an outside or other to it. And in *The System of Objects* and in both of those essays there is the whole problem of trying to write a *history* of simulation, to describe the progressive abstraction of the sign, when we are unable to say any more what comes before simulation, what lies outside of it.

But at the same time, even in the early work, we *can* see Baudrillard on occasion thinking through the methodological difficulties raised by his analysis, the way he must be at once inside and outside these systems of simulation. Though he rarely speaks of methodological issues in his work – it is only in interviews he does this – we are nevertheless able to read certain moments of his texts as allegorical of his own position as analyst. Take, for example, Baudrillard's characterization of the second order of simulacra in 'The Orders of Simulacra' as 'rather inadequate as an imaginary solution to the problem of mastering the world', 'ephemeral', an 'episode' of less interest than either the first or third orders. It is this order, according to Baudrillard, that is the time of the last great analysts of simulation, Walter Benjamin and Marshall McLuhan, at the cusp between the end of the Industrial Revolution and the beginning of that era we are currently in:

> The analyses of Benjamin and McLuhan are situated on these limits of reproduction and simulation, at the point where referential reason disappears, and where production is no longer sure of itself. In this sense they mark a decisive progress compared to the analyses of Veblen and Goblot. These latter, describing for example the signs of fashion, still refer to the classical configuration: the signs constitute a distinct material, have a finality and use for prestige, status and social differentiation. They manifest a strategy contemporaneous to that of profit and merchandise with Marx, at a time when you could still talk about the use-value of a sign or of force-of-work, when purely and simply one could still talk about an economy because there was still a Reason of the sign, and a Reason of production. ('OS', 102)

What Baudrillard is saying here, without saying it, is that Benjamin and McLuhan are privileged analysts of simulation because at this moment of the second order of simulacra they are at once before and after, inside and outside, simulation. They come after the initial freeing-up of the sign in the first order of simulacra, so they are able to observe its effects. But they also come before the sign's final liberation in the third order of simulacra, when nothing remains outside of it and there is no perspective on it. But this privileged moment can only be 'imaginary', 'ephemeral', an 'episode', because it would be impossible, that paradoxical moment of criticism itself. And this moment would always be the place of the analyst for Baudrillard, Baudrillard's own position (despite it notionally having passed), a point at once before and after, inside and outside, at the 'point' or 'limit' of simulation in a complex 'double strategy'.[7]

Consumer Society

We might, however, give a more detailed account of Baudrillard's thinking of the limits to these systems that have no limits by looking at another of his books, *Consumer Society*. *Consumer Society* was published before 'The Orders of Simulacra' and 'The Precession of Simulacra', which shows that what we are speaking about here is not a simple progression in Baudrillard's work but the way that each of his texts can be read as both a 'good' and a 'bad' thinking of simulation, a naming of an outside to simulation and an admission that we cannot name such an outside. *Consumer Society* is a continuation of *The System of Objects*, and particularly the last section there on the 'socio-ideological' system of consumption. In that section Baudrillard looks at how, if the individuality of different objects is produced by the system itself, then so too is their corresponding need or desire. He pays special attention to advertising and credit as two means for bringing about this desire, for ensuring there is always more demand than the goods available to satisfy it. *Consumer Society* continues this investigation into the creation of desire, this time not so much as the production of extra demand but as the contraction of the goods available to service existing demand. *Consumer Society*, that is, is an examination of the role of *waste* in contemporary society, a theme that is to run explicitly through all of

Baudrillard's work at least up to *Symbolic Exchange*. Waste or *dépense*, of course, is a notion that comes from Georges Bataille and, before him, from the anthropologist Marcel Mauss; and commentators have not been slow to pick up this lineage. Julian Pefanis, for example, in his *Heterology and the Postmodern: Bataille, Baudrillard and Lyotard*, writes: 'We could say that Baudrillard's critique of the systems and modes of productivist thought are filiated, via the agency of the situationists and the critique of the spectacle, to Bataille's analysis of modes of *dépense*' (1991: 54). And Baudrillard himself in interviews even speaks of this legacy (*BL*, 21, 166). But if waste is a theme in Baudrillard's work, and if it is what he mobilizes against simulation, then we must try to understand it in that double sense we have been attempting to develop. This waste is real, an empirically existing object that can be named as such; but it is also unreal, only stands in for what cannot be named. It is at once only that other to the system which helps it to expand and the very limit to this logic itself. In other words, we must ask: to what extent does waste remain specific to Bataille and to what extent is it a response to problems raised by the systems Baudrillard analyses? For waste becomes a *metaphysical* term in Baudrillard, abstract, unreal, doubling. This is the ultimate development in his work that we can see taking place in *Consumer Society*.

What is the usual economic understanding of waste? It is held that waste is something outside consumption, what inhibits consumption and what consumption must seek to overcome. Baudrillard in his book, however, inverts this economic common sense. For him, as we suggest, consumption is not about matching a pre-existing desire to a particular set of objects. Rather – and this is part of his brilliantly inventive rereading of the work of the psychoanalyst Jacques Lacan – consumption is not possible without a certain *excess* of desire over the object; or if desire is satisfied by the object, there is always another or an extra desire produced by this. Consumption in this sense is always incomplete, always involves or brings about a certain loss or absence. There is no way to bring consumption and the objects available to satisfy it into balance:

without this lack consumption would not occur at all. Indeed, we might even say that it is this very loss or waste which precedes consumption, that we would not desire anything without this waste. (This is as Baudrillard argues, following Mauss's work on the Pacific Islander phenomenon of 'potlatch', that it is not some basic level of biological existence that determines what can be wasted, but what can be wasted that determines this basic biological level: 'It is this "something in it more than itself" by which a thing becomes what it is "in itself". This is the law of symbolic value, which ensures that the essential is always beyond the indispensable' [*CS*, 51].) As an example of what he is saying, Baudrillard looks at the role of taxation in modern capitalist societies. Taxation is always thought of as a way of righting the inequalities of society, of the government playing a role in the fairer distribution of income – and, in the case of indirect taxation, of turning spending away from such socially undesirable ends as unnecessary imported goods, harmful and addictive substances, etc. However, Baudrillard asks, despite centuries of this taxation, have any of these aims actually been achieved? He answers, citing a French Planning Commission Report, no (*CS*, 38). But, as opposed to the Commission, this is not because the current method of taxation is inefficient or needs to be reformed. Rather, it is just in this inefficiency that it serves its purpose. It is exactly through imposing restrictions on the possible satisfaction of wants, in maintaining the distinction between classes, in making certain forms of consumption dangerous or anti-social, that taxation works to make consumption meaningful. (It is this which the bureaucrats cannot admit.) In fact, we might even say that not only does taxation maintain existing needs and the distinctions between classes, but it makes them possible from the very beginning. Tax does not levy a consumption that exists before it, but consumption comes about as an effect of this tax. Tax comes before the very consumption it taxes. Thus, if in one way tax redoubles pre-existing inequalities, in another way, as Baudrillard reminds us, these inequalities would not exist before they were redoubled (*CS*, 38).

We see the same thing in terms of production (and production and consumption are no longer simply opposed in consumer society: just as consumption has to be produced, so production is a form of consumption). Baudrillard begins by noting that in the calculation of the Gross Domestic Product of France not only are the goods actually produced counted as credits but also the expenses incurred during this production (*CS*, 46). The transportation costs involved in bringing goods to the market, in disposing of the leftover residues of the industrial process, in ridding the air of pollutants – all of these are counted as things produced! Of course, at first sight, as with tax, this seems wrong. These items should be counted as debits not credits and deducted accordingly from the National Budget. But Baudrillard points out that the National Accounts keeper is not mistaken here. For it is true that the waste brought about by production allows the possibility of further production. Indeed, we might even say that in the current anti-technology, pro-environment circumstances of the third order of simulacra we never actually have production as such but only waste – a waste, however, that is only possible because of production, that can only lead to further production (*CS*, 35–56). As with taxation, we might say that waste comes before production, that it is only the waste brought about by production which allows this production in the first place. Or to put it another way, things just as they are *doubled* by the assumption of production (*CS*, 46). The clean, natural, unaffected world is henceforth only conceivable as a result of the double process of waste and the clearing up of waste, production and the clearing up of production – a process which does not take us back to zero or add up to nothing but gives birth to production out of nothing, means that everything is only explicable in terms of production, that there is no other to production.

This, then, is the problem Baudrillard confronts in *Consumer Society*. He wants to think waste as the outside to the system of consumption. But at the same time what is shown is that it is this waste which the system produces, this waste which keeps the system going. This is why Baudrillard neither rejects waste – this would only be to make of him an economic liberal like

John Kenneth Galbraith (*CS*, 63–4) – nor, as many of his commentators would have it, simply asserts it – as Baudrillard himself says, the 'discourse of anti-consumption is now part of consumption itself' (*CS*, 315). Rather, the difficulty of speaking against the system of consumption is that, like the trade mark or brand name which is its emblem, there is nothing outside of it by which to judge it. It is beyond true and false, a kind of 'self-fulfilling prophecy' (*CS*, 197).[8] That is, it is not so much a matter of thinking the limits to the system of consumption as of thinking the consequences of it having no limits. What happens when waste is not simply outside but also inside the system? What are the paradoxical effects of the fact that, because of waste, there is no waste? Again, it is in light of these questions that we must evaluate Baudrillard's taking up of Bataille's and Mauss's notion of *dépense* in *Consumer Society*. It is to understand that it cannot only be waste in its substantialist and energetic sense, which is soaked up by the system, but also the limits to *this*. And we might try to make the complex distinction between these two different conceptions of waste clearer by turning to the last chapter of *Consumer Society*, 'Anomie in a Society of Abundance', to see how Baudrillard attempts to think there the limits to a system of consumption that has no limits.[9]

'Anomie in a Society of Abundance' is a chapter of *Consumer Society* its commentators have not known what to do with. It is mentioned by Kellner and Gane, but ultimately seen as nothing more than a series of journalistic '*faits divers*' tacked on to the end of the book, suggestive of a vague resistance to contemporary society. It seems very much a document of its time, a reflection of the drug and youth cultures of the late 1960s. But what is not seen is its systematic element, the way it is both a continuation of the arguments already put and a pointer to the future direction Baudrillard's work is to take. In this chapter, Baudrillard explores a certain form of violence that seems to mark modern consumer society, those solitary and infamous eruptions that have gone down in history: Richard Speck killing eight nurses in a hospital dormitory in South Chicago; Charles Whitman shooting 11 of his fellow students at the University of

Texas; riots and disturbances in Amsterdam and Montreal; and, of course, the brutal slayings of Sharon Tate and guests in the Hollywood Hills by the Manson Family (*CS*, 286–7). This is a new kind of violence, however, in that it is both 'without object' (*CS*, 279) and 'structurally tied to abundance' (*CS*, 285). In other words, it is not, as is usually the case, a protest against poor living conditions, but a protest against a *lack* of want, the *ease* of life, the fact that *nothing* is missing. And this resistance can take another form, this time anonymous and not so noticeable, harder to give instances of: 'fatigue' or 'passive refusal' (*CS*, 293), the rejection of consumption or the turning away from consumer society, as typified by the hippie or counter-cultural movements of the time.

But, crucially, these two alternatives – despite their initial appearance – are not mutually exclusive or even really contradictory. Rather, it is, as Baudrillard says, the very 'ambivalence' (*CS*, 293) between them, the possibility of exchanging one for the other, that is opposed to consumer society. It is the fact that the same group of people can alternate between violent attacks upon the system and a passive rejection of it that constitutes the specificity of their response and why consumer society finds it so hard to deal with. As Baudrillard says: 'Fatigue, depression, neurosis are always convertible into violence and vice versa' (*CS*, 293). In other words, it is the very *indistinguishability* between revolt and conformity that Baudrillard is in the end opposing to the system of consumption and not either one as such. It is this ambivalence and reversibility that the system can never finally reduce either to 'homoeopathic violence' or the 'luxurious sign' (*CS*, 284) of culpability. (It is for this reason that Baudrillard ultimately rejects both the terrorism of the first alternative and the passivity of the second, for the first becomes only a spectacle to be once again incorporated into the system and the second is only the 'inverse and complementary image' [*CS*, 289] of the social, the 'sentimental resurrection' [*CS*, 290] of the human.)

But what exactly does Baudrillard mean by this simultaneity of abundance and anomie, violence and passivity – and why is it this simultaneity rather than either one as such that he opposes to the system of consumption? In order to answer this question, we must turn to an earlier section of the chapter, where Baudrillard speaks of the relationship between 'anguish' and 'solicitation' (we might say therapy) in our modern societies of consumption. Again, it is an anguish, like the violence and passivity we see above, that arises not from natural want but from a 'rupture in the ambivalent logic of desire and thus the loss of the symbolic function' (*CS*, 284). That is, it is an anguish that arises not because our desires are unsatisfied but because they are *fulfilled*, because we have nothing left to desire. And it is a 'solicitation' that responds to this 'anguish' in either one of two ways:

> 1. For the one part, it attempts to re-absorb this anguish by the proliferation of varieties of solicitude: treatments, procedures, innumerable collective services – to inject everywhere a pacifying, succouring, deculpabilizing psychological lubrication [. . .]. A larger and larger budget is spent to console these 'miracles' of abundance for their anxious satisfaction.
> 2. Society tries – and in a systematic fashion – to recuperate this anguish as an opportunity for consumption, or to recuperate this culpability and violence in their turn as merchandise, as easily consumable, or as distinctive cultural signs. [. . .] Whatever, violence and culpability are mediated by cultural models and return as pre-consumed violence. (*CS*, 284–5)

We appear to have the same circularity here as we saw earlier between waste and consumption and waste and production. The system of consumption leads to anguish, but it is an anguish that leads in turn to an increase in the system. It is on the basis of this anguish that a whole new range of therapies and social services is instituted, a new set of experiences and images made over into media models. We can even imagine, as in the third order of simulacra, that normal, positive society is never seen as such but only in the form of this anguish – an anguish, however, which calls up this society and leads to its expansion. In a sense, therefore, as with production, there is no limit to the system of consumption. Even its other, anguish, is only possible because of it, brings about an increase in it. And yet what we can also see here is Baudrillard trying to think the limits to *this*. For this anguish arises not directly from want or lack but because there is no want or lack. That is, the very process of getting rid of it is also what causes it. If anguish is always being soaked up by the system, it is this soaking up itself which leads to anguish. In this regard, we would say that anguish – like waste – means that the system is always expanding, there is no limit to the system, but also that the system is never complete, has a limit. It is the limit that allows the system to have no limit. Anguish is ineradicable because its soaking up is only possible because of it, only leads to more of it. The very fact there is no anguish is only possible because of anguish, only brings about more anguish.

Waste, therefore, is not simply other to or outside of the system. It is not an external limit to it. Rather, it is an *internal* limit to the system, not so much before or outside of it as simultaneous with it. And if Baudrillard speaks of waste, both here and elsewhere, in terms of reversibility, it is at least in part in this sense: the fact that after a certain point in its progression, the system begins to reverse upon itself and the soaking up of waste leads to more waste. This is why Baudrillard insists on the structural law of waste as against all economic morality (even that which would make waste a part of the system). It is only by being less than totally efficient that the system runs well; and when the system runs too well and there is no waste, then the whole system becomes a form of waste. This is how Baudrillard is able to challenge the tautology of consumer society, the fact that it can only be taken up in its own terms. It is not by directly contesting it or proposing an other to it, but by asking what allows this self-definition or tautology, what is excluded to bring it about. It is to think – in almost another tautology – that the very self-definition of the system, and even the fact that waste is only possible because of it, is only possible because of waste. It is to think that at the very moment the system of consumption has no limit, excludes nothing, it precisely excludes waste. It is the circularity we see in that passage above and that we will see in a moment in *In the Shadow of the Silent Majorities*: the possibility that all of the resources of society are devoted to absorbing the anguish brought about by the fact that all anguish is absorbed by society.

It is at this point that we return again to the fundamental paradox that underpins *Consumer Society*, which is the fundamental paradox of the sign, consumption's entry – like objects – into the field of the sign. What is this paradox? It is that, if the comparison opened up by the sign (the fact that every object can be compared to another, that our desire is given to us by way of another) means that everything can be consumed, that nothing is outside the system of consumption, it also means that nothing can be consumed, that everything is outside the system of consumption, insofar as we never actually consume anything as such but only insofar as it resembles another, as it resembles the desire of another. In other words, if the fact that everything can be compared in terms of the sign means that there is nothing outside consumption, it also means that nothing is actually consumed because it is only consumed as something else, only consumed as another's consumption. And both that violence and passivity Baudrillard speaks of in 'Anomie in a Society of Abundance' are an attempt to respond to this. Violence wants to break through the mediation of the sign, to express or consume outside of the presence of the other. Passivity acknowledges that, insofar as consumption is only possible through the other, consumption is in fact impossible. Each of these solutions is inadequate by itself. The consumption of violence only turns into the non-consumption of the image of violence. The non-consumption of passivity, as Baudrillard has already demonstrated in the second section of *The System of Objects*, is only another, more refined version of consumption. And yet, taken together, in their ambivalence, reversibility and exchangeability, the fact that each becomes the other, they gesture towards the fundamental and essential limit of consumption: the fact that in the very act of consumption itself something goes missing; that the very thing – the sign – that allows, indeed, forces, us to consume also means that we cannot, that there is nothing to be consumed.[10]

In the Shadow of the Silent Majorities

We can see Baudrillard taking all this up in his later *In the Shadow of the Silent Majorities*. *In the Shadow* is not a book often linked with *Consumer Society* – the exceptions being the French sociologist Simon Langlois (1986) and the British media analyst Nick Stevenson (1995: 149–61) – but we can clearly read it as a continuation of *Consumer Society*'s arguments concerning the circularity between waste and consumption, solicitation and anguish.[11] More specifically, we can see in *In the Shadow* an elaboration of *Consumer Society*'s understanding of waste as both that other produced by the system that allows it to expand and the limit to this very logic. The role of waste in *In the Shadow* is played by what Baudrillard calls the 'masses'. Who or what are these masses? Before all else, the masses are the underclasses of society, all those whom the social attempts to inform, educate, inoculate. They are what the social justifies itself on the basis of. They are what all theories of sociology assume as their object of knowledge. They are what all systems of politics seek to mobilize or make active (*SSM*, 10). And yet, after centuries of doing so, the masses still remain to be socialized, are just as unknown and under-represented as before. After years of trying to get rid of them, there are more masses than ever. Now, we can say – and this is what all political, educational and administrative classes do as a way of defending their existence – that this is because up until now not enough resources have been devoted to the problem, or that these resources remain badly distributed. But, as in *Consumer Society*, Baudrillard draws a more radical conclusion (*SSM*, 11). These masses are not a contingent problem, something that goes against the social. Rather, the social itself produces these masses and is only possible on their basis (and thus it has no intention of getting rid of these masses or indeed any ability to do so). The masses still remain after years of the social not despite but exactly *because* of the social.

Baudrillard explores this daring hypothesis in the chapter '. . . Or the End of the Social' of *In the Shadow*. He begins by taking up there the notion that the social works through a kind of waste, the postulation of a certain other to it: 'Thus one sees the social expanding throughout history as a "rational" control of residues and a "rational" production of residues' (*SSM*, 73). That is, the social works both by soaking up that surplus value or waste which is capable of ruining our sense of worth and by producing a waste which itself needs to be soaked up. This is why direct opposition to the social is pointless. The social lives on the necessity of these 'others', these marginal or excluded groups. The direct refusal of the social only calls up all of the social's treatments of therapy, solicitation, deterrence, dissuasion, etc. As Baudrillard stresses, what he is proposing has nothing to do with those 'marginal defections' from the social in which revolutionary potential was seen by such theorists as Deleuze and Guattari in their *Anti-Oedipus*, the 'mad, women, druggies, delinquents', which, on the contrary, only 'supply new energy to the failing social' by producing more remainders for the system to absorb or socialize (*SSM*, 72). (And with this Baudrillard would also undoubtedly reject cultural studies readings of 'popular resistance': the taking up and turning against themselves of elements of the dominant ideology, although, perhaps to the surprise of both, we can see a number of affinities between them.[12])

At first sight, the masses would appear to be no different from these kinds of remainders. It is on the basis of their indifference, their refusal or unwillingness to be socialized, that the social persists, finds a role for itself. It is because of the masses, the fact that there are always more and more masses, that the social is able to continue expanding. The masses, as in the third order of simulacra, act as *a contrario* proof of the system of the social. If we never actually have the social as such but only the masses, these masses are finally only possible because of the social, only lead to a further increase in the social. And yet, as in *Consumer Society*, something paradoxical occurs as a result of this soaking up of all waste. At this point there perhaps arise the masses in Baudrillard's second sense. It is no longer the masses that are part of the system, a cycle within the system, but the system that becomes part of a wider cycle involving the masses. As Baudrillard writes in '. . . Or the End of the Social':

> Designated as refuse on the horizon of the social, [these remainders] thus fall under its jurisdiction and are fated to find their place in a widening sociality. It is on these remainders that the social machine starts up again and finds support for a new extension. But what happens when everybody is socialized? Then the machine stops, the dynamic is reversed, and it is *the whole social system which becomes residue.* As the social progressively gets rid of all of its residue, it becomes residual itself. By placing residual categories under the rubric 'society', the social *designates itself as remainder.* (SSM, 75)

What does Baudrillard mean by this? As we say, it is on the basis of the masses that there is no limit to the social, that everything is part of the social. Any outside to the social is only what the social produces, only leads to the further development of the social. And yet, as with the relationship between 'anguish' and 'solicitation' in *Consumer Society*, it is just this which also brings about the masses, for the masses are precisely the effect of this over-socialization, the collapse of the distinction between the social and its other. The social, that is, only ever existed as the 'critical and speculative distance between the real and the rational' (*SSM*, 84) in the second order of simulacra, but it is now this distance that is disappearing in its immediate '"blowing-up" and desperate staging' (*SSM*, 85) in the third order. This is the real reason why the social does not get rid of its remainders: because the very completion of the social leads to more remainders; because the social only lives on insofar as there are remainders. In a repetition almost of the argument used against the tautological structure of consumer society, we would say that, if the remainder is only possible because of the social, the social is only possible because of the remainder. Or, more acutely, we would say that the circularity between the social and remainder, the ability of the social to prove itself via the remainder, is only possible because of the remainder, only leads to another remainder. The masses in this sense are not simply outside or other to the social – if this were the case, they would be merely another 'marginal defection' from it – but the social is complete, there is nothing outside of it, only because it excludes the masses. The masses are not an *external* limit to the social, which the social would overcome, but an *internal* limit, a limit the social could never overcome, because it is a limit brought about by this very overcoming.

This, finally, is Baudrillard's complicated position on the masses, which we can see as the culmination of a long line of argument stretching back to *Consumer Society*. The masses are at once that limit posited by the social and that limit which allows the social to posit its own limit. They are at once what means that the social has no limit and the limit to *this*. But if the masses are the limit to the social as a system of simulation, they are also the limit to Baudrillard's own theory as a similar system of simulation. If they are excluded by the system's attempt to name them, they are excluded as well by Baudrillard's. That is, if, on the one hand, Baudrillard has to name the masses as a limit to the system of the social, on the other, he must also know that he cannot name them, that he would name them only to return them to the very system to which they are opposed. And again it is in relation to this double necessity or 'double strategy' – a term which comes from *In the Shadow* – that we would judge Baudrillard. For instance, as in 'The Precession of Simulacra', Baudrillard, despite understanding that saying the masses are outside of the social only leads to the further expansion of the social, still wants to argue of the social's attempt to make the masses speak: 'But it is too late. The threshold of the "critical mass", that of the involution of the social through inertia, is exceeded' (*SSM*, 23). Or, more subtly, he wants to assert alternately that the masses precede the social – 'the only referent which still functions today is that of the silent majority' (*SSM*, 19) – and that the masses are only a simulation of the social – 'all contemporary systems function on this nebulous entity, on this floating substance whose existence is no longer social, but statistical, and whose only mode of appearance is that of the survey' (*SSM*, 19–20) – without realizing that the real quality of the masses is that they are *both* simultaneously: that the masses are both that real which precedes the social and only a simulation produced by the social, both what is brought about by the social and what always remains for the social to soak up.

On the other hand, however, we can find moments where Baudrillard *does* think through the fact that the masses are not simply the end of the social but at once what makes the social possible and impossible, that the masses are not outside of or opposed to the social but also arise because of it. For instance, he does not choose between the three different hypotheses he puts forward concerning the effect the masses have upon the social throughout the book: (1) that 'the social has basically never existed' (*SSM*, 70); (2) that 'the social has really existed, it exists more and more' (*SSM*, 72); and (3) that 'the social has well and truly existed, but it does not exist any more' (*SSM*, 83), realizing that in a way these are indistinguishable, that it is only because the social never existed, excludes the masses, as in hypothesis 1, that it is able to be completed, as in hypothesis 2; or that it is completed, as in hypothesis 2, only to bring it to an end, as in hypothesis 1. And that both of these are as in hypothesis 3, which suggests not merely that the social once existed and now does not, but that it at once exists more and more, as in hypothesis 2, and never existed, as in hypothesis 1. This is why Baudrillard is able to say, as at the end of *Consumer Society*, that the specific response of the masses is a simultaneous resistance and conformity. The masses are not only outside the social, do not simply resist the social, but are also *in* the social, conform to the social, bring about its end by always wanting more of it. (The social collapses beneath the incessant demand for more medicine, education, welfare, etc.) Again, it is the very completion or perfection of the social that corresponds to its end, or its end that allows its completion. This is why in the second essay that makes up *In the Shadow*, 'The Implosion of Meaning in the Media', Baudrillard speaks of the masses not as the end or death of the social but as its 'catastrophe' (*SSM*, 103) or 'curvature' (*SSM*, 104) in the sense of its folding back onto itself, the fact that beyond a certain point subsequent improvements in the social lead to its demise, not to fewer but to more masses. And Baudrillard even thinks that, insofar as the masses are in part outside the social, there is nothing we can say about them, they are beyond the horizon of meaning. The masses here are unrepresentable, and they and their effects can only be assumed, remain hypothetical. This finally is the thing that needs to be remembered about the masses: they are not simply real, a sociological or even theoretical phenomenon, but a pure creature of representation, the power of language to change or double the world. For, in a sense, there are no masses, we never see the masses. There is only the social, the social soaking up the masses, but this only because of the masses, this only to be explained because of the masses. The absence of the masses is their proof, just as Baudrillard is suggesting here that the fact the social does not end, that there is no final collapse and breakdown, is the very evidence it has ended. We will return to this aspect of *In the Shadow* in Chapter 3.

The Transparency of Evil

The last text we look at here in the context of simulation is *The Transparency of Evil*. The subtitle of *The Transparency of Evil* is 'essays on extreme phenomena', and by this Baudrillard means both the extreme attempts of simulation to represent and master the world and the extremes that rise up against it, the contrary and unintended consequences that are produced as a result of its systems being pushed too far. In the book, as examples of this simultaneous extremity, there are essays on such topics as the omnipresence of art and the end of aesthetics (*TE*, 14–19), instantaneous world-wide information and computer crashes (*TE*, 36–43), and the improved effectiveness of antibiotics and the increased virulence of diseases (*TE*, 60–70). If *The Transparency of Evil* is published a long time after *Consumer Society* and *In the Shadow*, that is, it is still nevertheless trying to think the same question as them: what are the limits to systems that appear to have no limits? But this is perhaps asked with much more of a sense of the difficulty of the analyst's position *vis-à-vis* these systems, or at least an uncertainty as to whether it would be possible to name such a limit. Baudrillard knows here that he cannot say that the system crashes or comes to an end, that this end could only be envisaged in terms of the system, that its internal limit or 'catastrophe' would arise before this end. And, along these lines, he begins to think (a line of reasoning that goes all the way back to *The System of Objects*, where Baudrillard spoke of the practitioner of the system of objects being in a way a critic of it) the complicity between the critic and the system of simulation; whether it is his criticism which saves the system, prevents it from going too far, or indeed, inversely, whether it is the system which is ultimately its own critic, prevents itself from going too far, turns back on itself before it ends.

Let us pick up *The Transparency of Evil* at just that point where we left Baudrillard discussing the necessary circularity between a system and its other. The chapter 'The Fate of Energy' begins by retelling, as in *Consumer Society* and *In the Shadow*, Bernard de Mandeville's famous allegory *The Fable of the Bees* concerning the necessity for a certain waste, the way a system runs all the better for a little waste (*TE*, 102). Baudrillard then returns to that situation we saw in *Consumer Society*, in which there is a circularity between 'solicitation' and 'anguish', and *In the Shadow*, in which there is a circularity between the social and the masses, where a certain waste or remainder is produced but it is on this waste or remainder that the system starts up again. Or, to put it in its appropriately hyperbolic form, in which all the resources of the system are devoted to the soaking up of the waste or remainder produced by the fact that all waste and remainder is soaked up. Within this symbolic cycle of exchange and reversibility the system is able to run forever, always growing in size and yet never getting bigger or coming to an end. To use Baudrillard's favourite analogy at the time, it is like the perpetual motion machine of Alfred Jarry's *Supermale*, a bicycle that keeps on pedalling, even when its passengers are dead (*TE*, 102). Waste does not exist before production and production not before waste, but out of this exchange of each for the other something is produced out of nothing. Baudrillard calls it 'double or nothing'

(*TE*, 104). And he takes as an example of all this that pata-physical city New York:

> Consider New York City. It is a miracle that everything starts afresh each morning, bearing in mind how much energy has been used up the day before. The phenomenon is indeed inexplicable until one realizes that no rational principle of energy loss is at work here, and that the functioning of a megalopolis such as New York contradicts the second law of thermodynamics: the city feeds on its own hubbub, its own waste, its own carbon-dioxide emissions – energy arising from the expenditure of energy, thanks to a sort of miracle of substitution. (*TE*, 102)

This is the kind of 'extremism' Baudrillard is speaking of in *The Transparency of Evil*. A hyperproductive city like New York is in danger of becoming a pure simulacrum, of collapsing under its own perfection. But at this extreme point a certain limit is reached, and increased production, instead of simply producing more, brings about waste – a waste, however, on which the system starts up again. This is the true cycle within which the system operates, the proper exchange between the same and the other. It is a cycle we discovered at the end of *Consumer Society* and *In the Shadow*, in which, if the system produces its own waste or remainder and therefore there is no real waste or remainder, this is only because of, this only to lead to, another waste or remainder. It is to suggest that at the same time as the system expands, soaks up new remainders, it is also never completed, because there are always new remainders to absorb. But there is a difference of tonality between here and there. There it is nothing Baudrillard states explicitly and is always surrounded by an air of imminent crisis or collapse. Here it is this very economy which is Baudrillard's declared subject, and it is understood as the way things work 'after the orgy' (*TE*, 3). Indeed, Baudrillard argues, it is this cyclical economy that systems inevitably fall into, whether they intend to or not. It is the fact that, beyond a certain point, systems begin to reverse upon themselves, produce the opposite effects from those intended, that at once saves them and makes them possible from the beginning. If we can put it in a kind of paradox, it is the countervailing extreme phenomenon that occurs at the end of a system that forestalls an even worse eventuality, the possibility that it either fails or does not begin at all. It is a matter not of bringing the system up short, proposing some artificial limit to it – it is this, on the contrary, that leads to its end, that is a symptom of its end – but rather of forcing or following it to its furthest point, knowing that at this point the limit will arise that will prevent it from actually collapsing. As Baudrillard says: 'There is no longer any such thing as a strategy of Good against Evil, there is only the pitting of Evil against Evil – a strategy of last resort' (*TE*, 68; see also *TE*, 104).

But here we must be very careful – and this is where again it is a matter of reading Baudrillard closely and perhaps even against himself, judging him in terms of a necessary 'double strategy'. For, in speaking about the even worse fate that these 'extreme phenomena' save us from, Baudrillard wonders whether we are in fact to be condemned or saved by this. He asks, for example, in the later *The Perfect Crime*, in a rhetorical question that is to dominate his work from this time on:

> The only suspense which remains is that of knowing how far the world can derealize itself before succumbing to its reality deficit or, conversely, how far it can hyperrealize itself before succumbing to an excess of reality (the point when, having become perfectly real, truer than true, it will fall into the clutches of total simulation). (*PC*, 4)

But we would reply that in a sense this is a false alternative, that we cannot choose between the two possibilities, that they are both true and false. For what would the system derealizing itself to save itself from too much reality involve? It would be the attempt, as we saw with regard to the third order of simulacra, of the system to speak of something outside of it, to conjure up some other to it, an attempt which, as we have seen, is only to defer this real more than ever, is possible only because this real is already excluded, is just the hyperrealization of that second alternative. And what of this hyperrealization in turn going beyond this limit and falling into total simulation? It would only be the folding of the system back onto itself, its saving of itself before its final extinguishment, its ultimate derealization, as in the first alternative. We see the simultaneity of this derealization and hyperrealization, the end of the system and its carrying on after this end, in the following passage from *The Transparency of Evil*, which is also structured as a series of rhetorical questions:

Could it be that this suspension [of sex by AIDS] has a paradoxical aim, one bound up with the equally paradoxical aim of sexual liberation? We are acquainted with that spontaneous self-regulation of systems whereby they themselves produce accidents or slowdowns in order to survive. No society can live without in a sense opposing its own value system: it has to have such a system, yet it must at the same time define itself in contradistinction to it. [. . .] What if all this betokened a refusal of the obligatory flows of sperm, sex and words, a refusal of forced communication, programmed information and sexual promiscuity? What if it heralded a vital resistance to the spread of flows, circuits and networks – at the cost, it is true, of a new and lethal pathology, but one, nevertheless, that would protect us from something even worse? If so, then AIDS and cancer would be the price we are paying for our own system: an attempt to cure its *banal* virulence by recourse to a *fatal* form. Nobody can predict the effectiveness of such an exorcism, but the question has to be asked: What is cancer a resistance to, what even worse eventuality is it saving us from? (Could it be the total hegemony of genetic coding?) What is AIDS a resistance to, what even worse eventuality is it saving us from? (Could it be a sexual epidemic, a sort of total promiscuity?) (*TE*, 66)

Here again, it would be a matter of reading closely, both with and against Baudrillard. The first thing to note about this passage is how near all of this is to the third order of simulacra: the system as it were puts forward its own other to prevent an even worse fate, as we have seen it earlier proposing a certain real to exclude the real, waste to exclude waste, the masses to exclude the masses. But what Baudrillard is able to show in each case is how the system fails in its efforts to do so, how in its very attempt to speak of the real it becomes less real. We could in fact say that the system is only able to name or simulate the other because of the other, or that in trying to avoid the other it precisely brings it about. This is why ultimately there is no distinction between this objective law of the reversibility of the system, which we might call the symbolic or seduction, and the third order of simulacra. We have to say both that it is the system's ability to simulate the other that saves it from true simulation, means that the system reverses before it collapses, and that it is the very attempt to avoid this simulation by naming this other that brings it about, means an end to the system. But this is perhaps also why, against Baudrillard, we would say there is no distinction between those two fates he conjures up in that passage above: at once, simulation, in its self-reversal and auto-immunization as AIDS, avoids the worst fate, and this worst fate, insofar as it can be imagined at all, is only a projection of the system, a simulation of it like AIDS. It is not so much that there are two distinct and separate fates between which we must choose as that the same object, the same limit, always plays in two distinct registers, is at once the worst and the deferral of the worst. These are the two registers in which the key terms in Baudrillard's 'double strategy' play. They are both what in their naming is only a simulation of the system, an attempted deferral of its end, and what in being named help bring about that end of which they speak. Again, the third order of simulation would be indistinguishable from seduction in this regard: not only is its naming of the other an effect of the other, but it actually brings about that overturning of the system seduction and its necessary naming of a limit misses or avoids. But this is also why, if there is no outside to simulation, there is no inside to it either, why simulation never actually takes place. Against all realism, simulation remains unreal, hypothetical, only to be challenged by another hypothesis, seduction – and it is to seduction that we turn in our Chapter 2.

Notes

1. See also Norris, 'Lost in the Funhouse: Baudrillard and the Politics of Postmodernism' (1990), for an earlier version of this argument. Norris's reading of Baudrillard on the Gulf War is rejected by Paul Patton in his excellent translator's Introduction to *The Gulf War Did Not Take Place* (1995: 1–21).

2. See Jean-François Lyotard, *Libidinal Economy* (1993: 103–8) and David Wills, *Prostheses* (1995: 326). Bryan S. Turner has taken this question up in his 'A Note on Nostalgia' (1987).

3. Later, Baudrillard will distance himself from this historical project: 'I could have made a book out of it, others rushed in to find examples. As for myself, without denying it, I don't believe it holds up. For a time I believed in Foucauldian genealogy, but the order of simulation is antinomical to genealogy' (*BL*, 102).

4. That is, we might compare Baudrillard's arguments concerning simulation to the shift Foucault observes from the Renaissance order, based on 'resemblance', to the Classical order, based on 'similitude' (Foucault 1977a: 17–77).

5. See on this Baudrillard's discussion of the 'open' museum at Creusot, where the entire living working-class quarters is 'museumized' on the spot ('PS', 15–16) or the cloisters of St-Michel de Cuxa, which are first taken to New York and then returned to their 'original site' ('PS', 21–2).

6. See also *The Gulf War Did Not Take Place*, where Baudrillard speaks of a similar compact between America and Saddam Hussein to exclude the more radical potentiality of Islamic fundamentalism: 'People like him [Hussein] are necessary from time to time in order to channel irruptive forces. They serve as a poultice or an artificial purgative. It is a form of deterrence, certainly a Western strategy, but one of which Saddam, in his pride, is a perfect executant' (1995: 38).

7. In *Simulacra and Simulation* Baudrillard speaks of science-fiction as occupying this second order of simulacra, and more specifically as not 'opposing' the real, like the 'utopias' of the first order, but '*adding* the multiplicity of its proper possibilities' (*S and S*, 180–1) – or, as we will say later, *doubling* what is. And Baudrillard himself will often speak of his own work as a form of science-fiction (*EC*, 17; *BL*, 179).

8. See here Baudrillard's discussions of the 'tautological' and 'autoprophetic' nature of consumption (*CS*, 312–14), its self-referential 'mark' or 'brandname' (*CS*, 198), and the end of any 'transcendence' or critical position with regard to it (*CS*, 301–10).

9. See here the essay 'The Remainder' from *Simulacra and Simulation*, where two readings are possible: the first in which the remainder is simply a commutative other, what is left over after a certain subtraction; the second in which it is what is excluded to allow this very commutativity, what is left over when nothing remains.

10. See on this where Baudrillard says that the only thing consumed in our modern societies of consumption is the myth of consumption itself (*CS*, 311–12), that the object consumed is 'nothing' (*CS*, 316). In *America* also Baudrillard will conjure up the figure of a subject who is at once full and empty, consumes everything and nothing:

> The anorexic prefigures this culture in a rather poetic fashion by trying to keep it at bay. He refuses lack. He says: I lack nothing, therefore I shall not eat. With the overweight person, it is the opposite: he refuses fullness,

repletion. He says: I lack everything, so I will eat anything at all. The anorexic
staves off lack by emptiness, the overweight person staves off fullness by
excess. Both are homoeopathic final solutions, solutions by extermination.
(1988a: 39)

11. For essays connecting *In the Shadow* with Baudrillard's arguments on
simulation and the consequences of this for criticism, see Kuan-Hsing Chen,
'The Masses and the Media: Baudrillard's Implosive Postmodernism' (1987), and
Briankle Chang, 'Mass Media, Mass Mediation: Baudrillard's Implosive Critique
of Modern Mass-Mediated Culture' (1986).

12. For an essay relating Baudrillard's arguments concerning the masses to
the media theories of cultural studies pioneer John Fiske, see Deborah Cook,
'Symbolic Exchange in Hyperreality' (1994). See also Robert Dunn, 'Postmodernism, Populism, Mass Culture and the Avant-Garde' (1991) and Jim
Tarter, 'Baudrillard and the Problem of Post-New Left Media Theory' (1991).

2
Seduction

We turn now to seduction. It is possible to see seduction as the other principle that runs throughout Baudrillard's work, in parallel with simulation. What is seduction? In its dictionary definition, it refers to the act or action of causing a person to 'err in conduct or belief', to the 'leading astray' or enticement of another, particularly with regard to sexual matters. It is the getting of another to do what we want, not by force or coercion, but by an exercise of their own, though often mistaken or misguided, free will. The term is associated with a long line of great romances Baudrillard cites in his book *Seduction*: the myth of Don Giovanni; Choderlos de Laclos's *Dangerous Liaisons*; and Søren Kierkegaard's 'Diary of the Seducer'. It is a term that, as Baudrillard admits, derives from a previous aristocratic era, a time when there was a different relationship between the classes and sexes, which ended before the turn of the last century (*S*, 1; *BL*, 50). (Even in Kierkegaard's 'Diary of the Seducer', the term is ironic, affected, anachronistic, to use Kierkegaard's word, *aesthetic*. [Kierkegaard 1971: 7]) In this sense perhaps, it is a nostalgic concept, one whose applicability to the modern age might be questioned. And feminist and other critics of Baudrillard have not been slow to accuse him of perpetuating sexual stereotypes or, worse, advocating misogyny or even actual cruelty against women. For instance, the American literary theorist Jane Gallop writes: 'Baudrillard is, to my knowledge, the male French theorist who most explicitly and most frontally adopts an adversarial relation to feminism' (1989: 113). Or the British popular culture commentator Andrew Ross writes: 'Whatever is gained by [seduction] *in abstracto* is lost through Baudrillard's inability to recognize the urgency of a wide range of feminist strategies, crucial to a feminist politics' (1989: 217). And these are just a few of the generally unfavourable responses Baudrillard's notion of seduction has received.[1]

But, again, as with simulation, before reading Baudrillard in terms of some external real, before seeking to determine the social and political consequences of his arguments, it is necessary to read him in his own terms, to see how seduction operates in its original context. (This is not to say that seduction in Baudrillard's sense has nothing to do with its current usage. Rather, we would say that literal sexual seduction is only to stand in for, is at once allowed and disallowed by, Baudrillard's more abstract understanding.) The first thing to realize about seduction is that it is related to a series of other concepts in Baudrillard's work, with which it is more or less synonymous: symbolic exchange, waste, death, the masses, the fatal, illusion, theory. Each of these is specific and arises at a particular point in Baudrillard's career, but each is united in representing the opposite principle to simulation within that logic of representation we outlined in Chapter 1. That is, if simulation attempts to cross the distance between the original and the copy that allows their resemblance, seduction is both the distance that allows this resemblance and the distance that arises when this space is crossed. Seduction is the necessity of taking the other into account when trying to produce resemblance. It is that limit we cannot go beyond in our relationship to the other (another person, the real) if we still want to maintain a connection with it (*S*, 45–7). Indeed, against all interpretations of it as a form of sexual coercion, seduction is the idea that the other cannot be forced to follow, that in any such forcing there is always an ambiguity, a resistance possible by the other. Seduction is the idea that we cannot have a relationship without this undecidability, without it being impossible to determine whether it is we who lead the other or the other who leads us.

To this extent, we would say that seduction is opposed to simulation, for it is what means that simulation is never total, never able to account for the world, because it must always leave out the difference – the seduction – that allows this. And yet at the same time, seduction is not simply opposed to simulation, for it is also this difference that both allows simulation and ensures there is always more to simulate. We spoke in Chapter 1 about the way in which simulation is not just an empirical phenomenon that can be either confirmed or denied. As with the third order of simulacra, we never see simulation as such, but only its other – Indians in the forest, unspoilt or unpolluted nature – an other, however, that is only able to be seen in terms of simulation, that is its very proof. Simulation changes nothing in the world, but the world now can only be explained for an absolutely different reason. Simulation in this sense is not something real, but a hypothesis, an assumption that doubles the world. And against this no refutation is possible, no way of opposing something to it. Rather, we must, as it were, double simulation itself by a hypothesis which explains how it is possible, but only for a reason that completely goes beyond it. This is what seduction is. It is neither the same as simulation nor opposed to it, but *doubles* it. Simulation is henceforth possible, but only because of seduction. The resemblances it makes still occur, but only across the difference of, only to lead to, seduction. If seduction can only ever be seen in an always simulated form, this is only because of seduction itself. There is only simulation, but this only because of seduction.

But if seduction is never actually present, can only be grasped in an always simulated form, how then to write about it? In Baudrillard's work on simulation, as we saw, there was raised the question of the limits to systems attempting to resemble the world and even, as in the third order of simulacra, speaking of these limits. And this would apply to Baudrillard too in his own attempts to name the limits to those systems he is examining. But, as we also hoped to show, there is another

way of reading Baudrillard, as thinking not only why simulation
is never complete, never able to name its own limits, but also
why he could not himself name these limits, why they are
something that both he and the system would be subject to. It
is to admit that, if it is this difference that allows resemblance,
we could speak about it not directly but only indirectly, not
literally but only metaphorically. It is not something that
Baudrillard could point to in his work but something that is
embodied within it. And in a final paradox we would say that, if
seduction as that difference which allows resemblance can
never be represented, it is also implied in all representation. It
is a matter not of representing it, but of it allowing all representation (including its own). This is why Baudrillard can say
that seduction is both 'inextricable' (*BL*, 112) and 'inescapable'
(*S*, 42). It is always passing over into simulation and simulation
is always being seduced. And this is why we can always read
Baudrillard's text in two ways or against itself, both in terms of
simulation and in terms of seduction. Hence, if we have divided
our material here into two chapters, there is also no distinction
between them. We could read everything in Chapter 1 in terms
of seduction and all that follows in terms of simulation. But it is
this very inseparability between simulation and seduction that
is perhaps finally seduction.

The System of Objects

Accordingly, we might begin here by returning once more to
Baudrillard's *The System of Objects*. We have already looked at
The System of Objects, and particularly the section on objects
in their functional or objective register, in terms of simulation,
and made the point that objects in their non-functional or
subjective register are not essentially different because, just as
functionality pushed too far becomes non-functional, so non-
functionality can be a higher form of functionality. That is,
within the discourse of objects, the choice of deliberately
archaic or out-of-date materials can speak of a certain spirit of
make-do or improvisation, suggests a consumer who is thrifty,

capable of seeing the real value of things or all of whose needs are currently satisfied. Baudrillard gives the examples of a country house that is intentionally restored poorly by the architect so that it seems authentic (*SO*, 77–80) and of mass-produced craft that is crudely finished to appear hand-made (*SO*, 73–6, 84). That is, non-functional objects not only do not escape the rhetoric of functionality but are its highest achievement. Indeed, as in the third order of simulacra, we might even say that the non-functional realm of objects is precisely that limit put forward by the functional realm to prove itself all the more. Now, there is no outside to functionality, but only this 'non-functional'. The genuinely rustic and artisanal are henceforth only able to be seen as strategies within the discourse of functionality. It is perhaps for this reason – for this is before his formulation of simulation – that Baudrillard speaks of the relationship between the functional and non-functional orders as 'dialectical' (*SO*, 106).

However, there might be another way of reading Baudrillard at this point and of grasping what he means by 'dialectical' (or of understanding what he means by saying that the system of objects never finally reaches its 'dialectical' form [*SO*, 93]). It is to think the subjective order of objects not only as what ensures there is no outside to the objective order but also as its necessary other. It is to think that the subjective order is the attempt to take into account that limit which makes the objective order possible, that difference which allows its match between object and subject, function and need. How does it do this? As we have seen, the analogy between the system of objects and language is based on a certain notion of exchange they both share. With the increasing abstraction of objects, their being cut off from any external reality, the meaning of any particular item, like the individual component of a language, does not lie in itself (its use value) or even in its equivalence to some outside standard (its exchange value), but only in its relationship with other similar items (its sign value). Thus, in the painting of domestic interiors, we can choose any one colour only with regard to every other colour. Or in the decorating of these interiors, glass is the pre-eminent material because it is only the other objects viewed through it. We no longer want anything for what it is or what it can be used for, but only because somebody else wants it. But, if it is this comparison or exchange that allows us to say what anything is, what makes this comparison possible? If everything takes on its value only in relation to another, where did this value originate? What allows this system of signs to become closed and self-defining? To what are all these signs compared? It is the loss of this outside – let us call it the real – to which everything is compared that was at stake, we might recall, in the passage from the first to the second orders of simulacra, in simulation as such ('OS', 84–5). It is this outside or real which enables simulation that seduction allows us to think.

It is in the second section of *The System of Objects*, that devoted to objects in their non-functional or subjective register, that Baudrillard can be seen to be thinking the problem of this thing – the real – to which all else is compared, but which must itself be excluded to allow this comparison. That is, he begins to think the limits to that comparison or exchange which is necessary for simulation. What is the organization of objects in this non-functional or subjective register? As opposed to that first order in which objects are only compared to each other and have no outside, here they are always in a relationship with the one who owns them: they are 'possessed not used' (*SO*, 86). And perhaps the best example of this, the most profound expression of this subjective relationship to objects, is the collection. The important thing about the collection is not what is gathered together, its objective status in the world. Within the collection, even the most apparently functional objects, say 'carpets' or 'compasses' (*SO*, 86), are understood no longer in terms of any external use they might have, but only in terms of the place they occupy inside it. Even objects that are extremely common in everyday life, such as 'matchboxes' or 'cigar bands' (*SO*, 88), take on, as a result of the selection and discrimination implicit in the collection, a certain rarity. The unity of the pieces in a collection, that is, is not to be found in the objects themselves but only in the collector, because they all stand in for or express the subjectivity of the collector. Indeed, we might say that the ultimate stage of the collection is when it takes on the singularity of the collector him- or herself. That is, when as a result of the collector's taste and discernment, objects completely break with their outside function and reality and have only one quality linking them, one thing they have in common – the subjectivity of the collector. As Baudrillard says:

> The possession of a 'rare' or 'unique' object is obviously the ideal aim of its [subjectivity's] appropriation, but for one thing the proof that a given object is unique can never be supplied in a real world, and, for another, consciousness gets along just fine without proof. [. . .] Its absolute singularity, on the other hand, arises from the fact of being possessed by me – and this allows me, in turn, to recognize myself in the object as an absolutely singular being. (*SO*, 90)

But, as Baudrillard says here – and this is the paradox of the subjective register of objects – if the objects in the collection stand in for the subjectivity of the collector, this subjectivity does not exist before these objects. It is only to be seen through them. It is entirely constructed by them (*SO*, 91). There is thus a kind of circularity or aporia implied in the subjective order of objects. It is able to constitute itself, have an underlying unity, only on the basis of the subject, but this subject in turn is only to be given through its objects. In any account of the subjective order of objects, therefore, something is always missing, precisely that initial exchange of object for subject and subject for object by means of which each becomes what it is. And Baudrillard brilliantly connects this with the idea that the collection only exists, has meaning, insofar as a piece is missing from it – a piece he explicitly associates with the collector him- or herself. As he writes: 'Any collection comprises a succession of items, but the last in the set [which is always missing] is the person of the collector' (*SO*, 91). It is this missing piece that severs the collection from external reality, the functional order of objects, by making it less than it; but it is also this missing piece that allows the collection to resemble reality, the subjectivity of the collector, in its very difference from it. Put simply, it is through this missing piece that the rest of the collection exchanges itself. It is this missing piece that every other piece in the collection takes the place of (every piece in the collection *is* this missing piece, attempts to speak of what the subjectivity of the collector and the rest of the collection have in common), but each also defers this missing piece insofar as it can only take its place so long as it is excluded. This is the meaning of the anecdote Baudrillard retells from La Bruyère concerning a connoisseur who gives up collecting because he is unable to track down the final print in his collection, and in fact is willing to swap the rest of his collection for this piece; but who, when he finally does obtain it, soon loses interest in his collection because it is now closed, self-contained, no longer requires his subjectivity to be completed. As Baudrillard says: 'The equivalence experienced here between the whole series minus one and the final term missing from the series is conveyed with arithmetical certainty' (*SO*, 92).

All this is perhaps the true dynamic of the collection, its at once 'satisfying' and 'disappointing' quality (*SO*, 86). In one sense, a good collection is always moving away from any objective quality linking its components – this is too much like mere accumulation. The good collection instead has a difficult, hard to discern quality connecting its various parts. Ideally, it is something that can only be seen by the collector. And this is perhaps the true 'dialectic' of the collection. Each piece in the collection does not simply add to the ones before it, follow a pre-established rule. On the contrary, it attempts to be different from the other pieces, to sum up all that comes before it, adopt the position of the last piece of the collection – the subjectivity of the collector – that all the previous ones have in common. In other words, each additional piece in the collection seeks to draw out some new quality linking the others that has not been seen before. It adds something that at first does not seem like those others, but that in retrospect allows us to perceive a new commonality between them. It wants to show that the summing-up attempted by the previous piece was only partial, that though it was thought to end the series, to occupy a meta-position with regard to it, it is in fact only part of a larger series it does not see, is no different from the rest.

But this is also why the collection can never be completed. As we say, each new piece attempts to be the last piece in the collection, to be the single thing all the others have in common, to occupy the position of the subject; but insofar as it is able to do this, to be compared to those others in this way, it opens up the possibility of another piece coming after *it*, speaking of what *it* and the rest of the collection have in common. The collection as it grows gets closer to this condition of singularity, of having only one thing in common – we might almost say nothing in common – but the comparison that makes this possible also makes it impossible. The very thing that allows any particular piece to occupy the position of the subject also means that the subject is excluded, that the subject is what all the pieces have in common necessarily comes after it. However, we would say that the collection – the practice of collecting – is exactly an attempt to realize this, the *economy* of this failure. The pleasure of collecting – its at once 'satisfying' and 'disappointing' quality – is that each piece seeks to complete the collection and yet knows that it cannot, and does not even want to. The collector's pleasure grows the longer the collection continues and more and more ingenuity is required to obtain the next piece; but he or she also knows that at the same time the risk increases, that each new piece brings the conclusion closer, that moment when he or she will be unable to find another piece. The pleasure in collecting is inseparable from a certain risk or pain. Each piece in the collection stands in for the last piece, completes the collection, and also attempts to defer this end. Each piece in the collection is at once its end and the impossibility of its end.

This is the profound question of *time* implied in the collection. The 'habit' of collecting, insists Baudrillard, is not the simple 'regularity' or 'continuity' implied by that word, but rather a kind of simultaneous 'discontinuity and repetition' (*SO*, 94) – discontinuity because, as we have seen, in a good collection it is difficult to say how we get from one piece to another, there is no obvious rule to follow; repetition because, in retrospect, the rule was already there, any additional piece is not truly new but merely a continuation of the old. And along the same lines Baudrillard also disagrees with the characterization of collecting as a narcissistic striving for immortality through a self-reflection in objects: 'The refuge-seeking procedure depends not on an immortality, an eternity or a survival founded on the object *qua* reflection (something which man has basically never believed in), but, instead, on a more complex action which "recycles" birth and death into a system of objects' (*SO*, 96). Collecting is not narcissistic because, as we say, there is no preconstituted subject before its exchange for the object. Instead, in an impossible simultaneity – at once a discontinuity and repetition – both are born at once. A narcissism, a reflection between the collector and his or her objects, is perhaps produced, but only across a void or gap – precisely the 'subject' itself – which at once precedes exchange and is produced by it, is what exchange stands in for and is left over after it. This is why Baudrillard says that it is not so much immortal life as death that is at stake in collecting, for every exchange takes the place of the subject, every exchange *is* the subject; and the subject is always excluded, we always need another exchange to say what the subject is. The subject at once is always given, nothing but its exchange with the object, and excluded to allow this, the very thing that enables the exchange of subject for object. Like the cyclical or circular time that is involved in the habit of collecting, it is because the subject is at the beginning of the collection, common to all pieces, that it is missing, that we cannot say how to get from one piece to another. It is because all objects can be compared that we can ultimately have an infinite distance between them (it is because we can compare the objects in a collection that we can endlessly add new ones, until all the various items in the collection have nothing in common); and this infinite distance would only be possible because they all have something in common (we can never actually get to that final state of the collection where there is only one single quality connecting all the various pieces because we could do this only insofar as we were able to compare them, a comparison that always implies another). But in all of this again the collection is itself the thinking of, the grappling with, the paradox of something at once incomparable and infinitely compared that allows comparison, the simultaneous discontinuity and repetition that allows linear accumulation. We might say the seduction that allows simulation.

For a Critique of the Political Economy of the Sign

We can see the same problem of exchange at stake in another moment in Baudrillard's work, the essay 'The Art Auction: Sign Exchange and Sumptuary Value' in *For a Critique of the Political Economy of the Sign*. *For a Critique* is an important book for Baudrillard. It is where he tries to formalize the intuitions regarding the sign in his two previous books, *The System of Objects* and *Consumer Society*. In particular, it is where he begins to think through for the first time the consequences of symbolic exchange, how it cuts against both use and exchange values. As Gary Genosko says in his *Baudrillard and Signs*, perhaps the most detailed study of *For a Critique*: 'Symbolic exchange is the other side of political economy. One crosses over to it from use value and sign value by means of a symbolic consumption which liquidates value' (1994: 10). But what must also be understood is that, if symbolic exchange subverts use and exchange values, it is what makes them possible as well. Baudrillard raises this as a kind of contradiction here, something he does not want to address or even acknowledge, but it is undoubtedly part of what he is saying: 'The objects involved in reciprocal exchange, whose uninterrupted circulation establishes social relationships, annihilate themselves in this continual exchange without assuming any value of their own. Once symbolic exchange is broken, the same material is abstracted into utility value, commercial value, statutory value' (*PE*, 125). However, we see nothing wrong with this – and the subsequent development of Baudrillard's work bears this out. Symbolic exchange in that sense we were trying to bring out at the end of Chapter 1 is not simply the negation of economic value but rather its *limit*.[2] It is the thinking of that loss, that relationship to the other, which at once allows exchange, opens it up, and means that it is never complete, never able to account for itself.

This is pursued in an abstract way in *For a Critique* in the essay 'For a General Theory', where Baudrillard expresses it as a series of mathematical proportions, but we take it up in a more practical manner through Baudrillard's analysis of the art auction. Here too there is an investigation into the symbolic or sumptuary as both the origin and end of economic value. For, as Baudrillard says, what we have in the auction is a kind of 'crucible' (*PE*, 112) of capitalist exchange, a place where we can see value arising as such without the pretext either of use value (for a painting has no use) or exchange value (for it is the value of the painting that the auction is seeking to determine). In other words, what we see in the auction, as in the collection, is that moment *before* use and exchange value, that exchange before them that makes each possible. What takes place in the art auction? What is the clue it provides to the production of economic value? What we see in the art auction is that, before the consideration of need or the calculation of profit, there is a kind of 'reciprocal wager' (*PE*, 116) between its various parties, an 'aristocratic parity' between 'peers' (*PE*, 117) in which each is recognized in his or her difference. It is in this symbolic reciprocity in which each gives to the other without expectation of return that value is born. It is as a result of this impossible moment that exchange becomes possible, and that infinite regress in which everything only takes its value from another is overcome (and produced). But for Baudrillard this is also the *risk* implied in value and exchange. For it is always possible, if the other does not exist before our exchange with it, that there is no other with whom to exchange, that there will be no bid after ours, that our bid will not be returned. It is this which each party in the auction tries to take into account – like the collection, the auction is the *economy* of this risk – but it is also this risk that the auction reveals as necessary for the creation of economic value. Value only arises because we cannot say what the bids are for or what the object is worth. Value is inseparable from the loss or destruction of value. Baudrillard writes:

> The act of consumption is never simply a purchase (recon-
> version of exchange value into use value); it is also an
> expenditure (an aspect radically neglected by political
> economy as by Marx); that is to say, it is wealth manifested
> and a manifest destruction of wealth. It is that value,
> deployed beyond exchange value and founded on the latter's
> destruction, that invests the object purchased, acquired,
> appropriated, with its differential sign value. It is not the
> quantity of money that takes on value, as in the economic
> logic of equivalence, but rather money spent, sacrificed,
> eaten up according to a logic of difference and challenge.
> (*PE*, 112–13)

More specifically, what does Baudrillard mean here by 'value,
deployed beyond exchange value and founded on the latter's
destruction'? What is implied by money taking on value not
according to an 'economic logic of equivalence' but according
to a 'logic of difference and challenge'? In order to answer
these questions, let us consider the actual process of an auction
in more detail. As we say, if in some sense we know the value
of what we are bidding for before the auction, in another sense
what the auction reveals is that its value is not given before its
exchange. We might speak, for instance, of the 'aesthetic value'
(*PE*, 120) of a work of art as though this somehow justified our
bid, but it is difficult to imagine this rising throughout the
course of the auction as it appears to. Rather, of course, it is
the rising bids themselves that produce this increasing value.
The so-called 'aesthetic value' of the work is nothing but the
price willing to be paid for it (*PE*, 116, 117). And yet, as
Baudrillard says, it is not as though the money paid for the
work is worth anything before it is exchanged. It too is just as
useless, just as 'pure' (*PE*, 117), as the object for which it is
swapped. To an extent, then, what we see in the auction – as
Baudrillard stresses, unsupported by either use or exchange
values – is the production of value through the exchange of one
thing without value for another thing without value. What sign
and even exchange value stand in for, what makes each
possible, is this impossible 'aristocratic' exchange of two things
alike in their very difference. But what we also see in the
auction is that, if the origin of exchange is this symbolic

reciprocity, this exchange can never be grasped as such. We are always either too soon or too late for it. We are too late because, as we say, the various bids in an auction are the attempt to stand in for or take the place of an original exchange or value that seems to precede them. We are too soon because, as we have also seen, this exchange or value is only an effect of or only given by the very attempt to stand in for it.

We get an even clearer idea of this – of how economic exchange both depends upon and defers symbolic exchange – if we consider the actual process of bidding. For what really happens there? Two or more parties bid for the same object, each trying to predict its final value. But the final value of the object is affected by (and perhaps only an effect of) these very bids. In a sense, therefore, each bidder is not so much bidding for the object as trying to predict the relationship between others and the object. Each – like each additional piece in the collection – is not merely the next in the series but also attempts to sum up the rest of the series. But this also applies to his or her competitors. They too are not so much bidding for the object as trying to predict others' relationships to it. At once each bidder wants to beat the others, be the first to summarize the series, get his or her bid in before the auction-eer's hammer falls; and yet no one actually wants to be the first, each knows that his or her summary is only part of the series, that his or her bid merely opens up the possibility of another. Again, the paradox of the auction is that at once each party tries to stand in for the relationship between others and the object and this relationship would not exist before the attempt to stand in for it. Each bid seeks to grasp or make an equivalence between the self and the other, but this is only possible because of, this only leads to, a difference between them, another move or turn by the other that must be taken into account.

It is this which accounts for the strange rhythm of the auction, the importance of its specific tempo and circumstances (Baudrillard's word is *unicité* [*PE*, 116]). The time of the auction is not simply continuous but, with its sudden rushes of bids and its equally abrupt pauses, at once discontinuous and cyclical, unrepeatable and only able to be repeated. Within the ritualized space of the auction, there is no way of remaining outside or neutral: every gesture, even indifference, is already understood as an action, and the other has already responded on its basis. It is for this reason that we must act before the other does. And yet, as we have seen, we also do not want to act before the other but only after. It is this which accounts for the auction's various circuit-breaking mechanisms: at once a delaying of bids, a number of things that must be done before we can bid, and a forcing of bids, a time within which the bid must be made before the auction is over. It is this which attempts to resolve – but also what opens up – the temporal deadlock of the auction in which each party has already moved and no one wants to move. But, we might ask, what happens when the actual deadline does arrive in the auction, when the hammer falls and this potentially infinite back-and-forth between the various parties comes to a halt? How is this to be understood? In one sense, the process undoubtedly does stop when the hammer falls and the final price is given. But in another sense too, this end is deferred. For the object only has value insofar as its true value is unknown, insofar as it can be exchanged for something else, insofar as there is a bid after it. (This is why, as Baudrillard says, any profits or winnings accrued in the game can only be re-invested or gambled again, cannot be taken away from it without losing value [*PE*, 117].)

It is this that gets us toward the final strategy of the auction. The bids rise, we get closer to the final bid, but at the same time we do not ourselves want to make this final bid, when there is this definitive exchange between money and its object, the bidder and what he or she has bid for. And it is this relationship to the last bid that each of the parties in the auction tries to take into account, the fact that they do not want to make the last bid but always the one before, that they can make the last bid but only because there is another after it. Again, however, it is just this which the other also takes into account, and so on. That is, if there is a kind of counting forward from the first bid, each opening up the possibility of another after it, there is also a kind of counting back from the last bid, with each standing in for and deferring it. This is perhaps the final equivalence at stake in the auction. Just as we do not want to make the first we also do not want to make the last bid; but each bid as it were stands in for this last bid, which is also the first. Or, to express this by way of analogy with the collection, what every bid stands in for is the equivalence of the first and last bids (we only bid because of that initial exchange between money and the object which allows any bid; every bid seeks to put a figure on the final value of the object); but this bid is only possible because it is not the first or last bid, because the first and last bids are missing (we only bid after another; we only bid insofar as we think there is another after us). Every bid occurs across this impossible simultaneity, takes its place. But this equivalence itself – symbolic exchange – can only ever be seen in an already comparative, different form, always requires another comparison or exchange. Exchange, if it allows value, also means that we cannot say what anything is worth. Exchange, if it opens up value, is also its impossibility or end.

This is what Baudrillard means by the sumptuary, the fact that value is only possible on the basis of that 'aristocratic' reciprocality between two incomparables in which there is always a risk there is no first or last exchange. In everyday life, value always comes from another, but we ultimately cannot see where this other gets its value from. We never have exchange as such, but are always as it were in between exchanges. In the auction, however, we see the origin of exchange, how value arises on the basis of the impossible 'parity' between money and object, buyer and seller, in which each is given its value at once. The sumptuary is not the simple end of value – we could speak of this end only to stand in for it, exchange it, compare something to it – but rather we see that value is only possible on the basis of this end, that exchange is only undertaken with the chance there might be no more exchange. Every exchange is the attempt to stand in for that missing first exchange. Every exchange is the attempt to defer that last exchange. And the sumptuary is this simultaneity of value and the destruction of value. (We might say, as with the collection, that it is this equivalence of the beginning and the end, the first and the last exchange, value and the destruction of value, that means there is an infinite distance between them, that there is always another bid; but also that it is this infinite delay, the fact that we cannot know for sure whether any bid is the final one, that produces the possibility of their equivalence.) Against the generalized exchange of simulation, the paradox of aristocratic parity, the fact that in entirely risking ourselves we can induce and indeed force the other to exchange with us, is that both parties are alike in their absolute incommensurability. We are the same, but our equivalence is infinitely deferred; we are opposed, but everything stands in for our identity. We would say that the two parties in an auction are precisely in a rela-tionship of *seduction*. And we would say that the real aristocratic parity here, the one thing that is truly equal to itself alone, is the very medium of exchange itself: money or the painting. It is the single object which, in its difference from itself, in only ever being able to be grasped in a comparative form, everything wants to imitate or resemble. The medium of exchange – apparently the most low, the most lacking in value – is the true aristocrat of exchange. And perhaps another name for this medium of exchange – at once the lowest and the highest, infinitely compared and incomparable, the limit to the system of simulation and what the system endlessly displaces – is the real itself.

Baudrillard is thus able to argue in 'The Art Auction' that the whole economic system is based on this impossible exchange between value and the destruction of value that we see in the art auction. But at the conclusion of the article, he argues that in our contemporary world we are witnessing the decline of this sumptuary, losing touch with this enigma of value. We no longer have an aristocracy that does not measure itself in relation to other classes (and hence the aristocratic squan-dering of wealth), but only a parody of its sacrificial and risk-taking style. Our modern societies of simulation have repressed that seduction which lies at their heart. This is why Baudrillard must turn to such marginal activities as the art auction and gambling to see the last remaining vestiges of these sumptuary processes.[3] He writes:

> Something similar to this sumptuary exchange and this aristocratic model, but weakened and geared down, diffuses through the whole system of consumption and provides its ideological efficacy. It seems absurd to speak of a 'democratized' logic of caste. Yet consumption is instituted on the basis of the exchange of differences, of a distinctive material and thus of a potential community, which, however little remains of it – and precisely because nothing of it remains – is nevertheless articulated upon a fiction of aristocratic parity. The difference – a major one – between the aristocratic potlatch and consumption is that today differences are produced industrially, they are bureaucratically programmed in the form of collective models. They no longer arise in the personal reciprocity of challenge and exchange. Only the mass-mediatized simulacra of competition operate in the statutory rivalry. This latter no longer has the real, distinctive function that it still had in Veblen: the great dinosaurs of 'wasteful expenditure' are changed into innumerable individuals pledged to a parody of sacrificial consumption, mobilized as consumers by the order of production. (*PE*, 119)

But in fact against Baudrillard here – and as we saw earlier in *Consumer Society*, *In the Shadow* and *The Transparency of Evil* – there is no real alternative between these two destinies. To read Baudrillard's own argument carefully, there is no choice: this sumptuary is already its own 'democratization', allows its own 'gearing down'. We never see symbolic exchange as such, but only that sign value which stands in for it. But this simulation in turn is only possible because of the sumptuary. The very decline or absence of the sumptuary, therefore, is only possible because of it, is its very proof. There is no separating the two; they are simultaneous. But again it is this very simultaneity between value and the loss of value that is the sumptuary. The sumptuary *doubles* exchange. Baudrillard's article is entitled 'The Art Auction: Sign Exchange and Sumptuary Value', and it is this simultaneity before all else that must be kept in mind.

Fatal Strategies

There is one more essay here where we might see Baudrillard speaking of this 'aristocratic' sumptuary or medium of exchange. It is the chapter 'The Hostage' from the section 'Figures of the Transpolitical' in the book *Fatal Strategies*. In this chapter, Baudrillard looks at the terrorist taking of hostages and how it is used against modern society. Baudrillard has already spoken of terrorism, as we have seen, in *Consumer Society* and *In the Shadow*, and does so as well at the end of *The Mirror of Production*. Most commentators understand this terrorism literally, as though Baudrillard is speaking about or advocating actual armed insurrection. For example, *nouveau philosophe* Jean-Pierre Faye speaks of a 'nostalgia for a society of cruelty and terror' in Baudrillard's work (1985: 5). And in a way this is true. But also by this stage in his career – and arguably always in retrospect – Baudrillard's writing is consciously metaphysical. If terrorism inflicts real violence and death – and he is writing throughout the reign of political terrorism in Europe with the Baader–Meinhof Gang in Germany and the Red Brigades in Italy – its more profound aspect is the strange limit it reveals in the social in its efforts to defend itself from it. That is, if Baudrillard is interested in the phenomenon of hostage taking in 'The Hostage', it is not because it is simply antagonistic, a direct challenge to the social (as we will see, terrorism in this sense only strengthens the social), but because it is a moment, like the auction and perhaps even the collection, where we can see the constitutive limits to the social, that paradoxical 'beyond value' (*PE*, 122) that makes the exchange upon which it depends both possible and impossible. For the terrorist would take the hostage as the singular equivalent for the rest of society only to show that no one wants him or her, that he or she is worth nothing. As Baudrillard says: 'The hostage is himself obscene. He is obscene because he no longer represents anything. [. . .] This is verified by the impossibility of getting rid of him' (*FS*, 42–3). That is, the terrorist would take the hostage as an expression of his demands against society only to realize that this medium of exchange cannot itself be grasped or exchanged. And yet, as we will see, what terrorism also reveals – whether deliberately or not – is that the social is premised on the possibility of taking its own citizens hostage in the same manner, rendering everybody responsible for everybody else – an attempt which similarly fails. The social seeks to become a total principle, entirely to possess its subject, but what terrorism shows is that it can become total only because of another, that it can possess its subject only because it is able to exchange him or her for or with another.

Baudrillard begins 'The Hostage' with an account – an extension of the analyses in *Consumer Society*, *In the Shadow* and even 'The Orders of Simulacra' and 'The Precession of Simulacra' – of the progressive stages in the increasing 'security' (*FS*, 37) of the system of the social. It is a security precisely based on protecting its citizens from the possibility of outside threat as represented by something like terrorism. The first stage is a 'relatively loose, diffuse and extensive state of the system', producing 'liberty' (*FS*, 37). The second stage is a 'different state of the system (denser)', producing 'security (self-regulation, control, feedback, etc.)' (*FS*, 37). The third stage is a 'further state of the system, that of proliferation and saturation', producing 'panic and terror' (FS, 37). In other words, we now live in a system in which everything is connected to everything else, everything is exchangeable for everything else. We live in a world of total order, total determination, in which every event must have an explanation or cause; but it is also a system in which for this reason the smallest action can produce the most extreme consequences, the most minute imbalance can set off the most destructive chain of events. (Baudrillard will compare this later in *The Illusion of the End* to that famous 'butterfly effect' in chaos physics, where the fluttering of a butterfly's wings on one side of the world can set off a hurricane over on the other side [*IE*, 110]). Baudrillard writes:

> Because there is no longer a responsible subject, each event, even a minimal one, must be desperately imputed to someone or something – everyone is responsible, some maximal floating responsibility is there, waiting to be

invested in any kind of incident. Every anomaly must be justified and every irregularity must find its guilty party, its criminal link. This too is terror and terrorism: this hunt for responsibility without any common measure with the event – this hysteria of responsibility that is itself a consequence of the disappearance of causes and the almighty power of effects. (*FS*, 36–7)

But, as Baudrillard suggests here, beyond a certain point in this process, increasing security, instead of protecting us against terror, in fact brings it about. Instead of offering an explanation for everything and relieving us of individual responsibility, modern security makes life random and incomprehensible, holds everyone responsible for everybody else. And it is a 'security' that contemporary terrorism – with its kidnapping of one hostage to strike at the whole system, its holding of one person as an embodiment of the evils of all of society – replays in its own way. That is, against a system in which everyone is hypothetically responsible for everybody else, everyone is exchangeable for everybody else, terrorism does indeed take someone and hold him or her responsible in this way, does try to exchange him or her for a whole series of demands against the state. Terrorism in this sense is not simply opposed to the social, but a kind of extrapolation or exaggeration of it. To the simultaneous responsibility and arbitrariness of the system, it responds with an even greater responsibility and arbitrariness; to the generality of the system, in which *most* of us are responsible for *nearly all* the others, it imposes an absolute singularity and universality, in which *everyone* is responsible for *all others*. As Baudrillard says:

This [the social's taking of us hostage] is an extreme and caricatured version of responsibility: an anonymous, statistical, formal and aleatory one that plays on the terrorist act of the taking of hostages. But if you think about it, terrorism is only the executioner for a system which seeks both total anonymity and, at the same time and contradictorily, total responsibility for each of us. With the death of anyone, it executes the sentence of anonymity that is henceforth ours, that of the anonymous system, anonymous power, the anonymous terror of our real lives. (*FS*, 36)

But at this point a question must be asked, for it is impossible to say which comes first here: terrorism or the social. On the one hand, the system justifies its security on the basis of terrorism. The terror of its security is only to prevent the even worse threat of terrorism itself. But, on the other hand, terrorism justifies its activity on the basis of a terrorism already operative in society. It is only in response to – as an 'executioner' of – a process already in society that its taking of hostages can come about. In a sense, therefore, each is only possible because of the other, only through its exchange with the other. In a way we have seen before, it is the very exchange between them that precedes either as such. For, again, on the basis of what is the security of the social instituted and able to increase, in fact to become, as in its third stage, infinite? Only, paradoxically, because of the continued threat of terrorism. It is only because the threat of terrorism remains that we are able to get to that stage where the security of the social has no limit, where the possibility of terrorism has been totally eliminated. And, inversely, how is terrorism able to continue in its efforts to destroy that society in which each is responsible for all, each exchanged for all? Only by taking a hostage and having that social, which understands itself as responsible for all, seek to exchange everything for it.

This is the ambiguity terrorism, a certain kind of terrorism, attempts to bring about. Each side – the social and the terrorist – tries to take us hostage in order to render everyone totally responsible, to see that one is exchanged for all, to make exchange transparent. But the paradox – the paradox that terrorism tries to bring about – is that at the very moment the hostage is least free, most bound by exchange, held responsible for the rest of society, he or she is most free, not bound by anything at all, unable to be exchanged for anything or with nobody to exchange with (*FS*, 47–8). That is, neither terrorism nor the social can go to the end in its efforts to take us hostage because we only remain hostage insofar as there is another outside of it with whom it can exchange. And this is perhaps the same as saying that in any attempt by terrorism or the social to account for itself, to exchange itself for everything, to render exchange visible, there is always one exchange left out – and that is that exchange between it and the other for which everything within it stands in. There is always a limit to any 'provocation' and 'manipulation' (*FS*, 40), whether that of terrorism or the social, always an exchange before it and after it. It is on the basis of this inexchangeable – individually responsible, free, independent – hostage that both begin their process of initiating exchange, but this exchange taken to its furthest reach also produces a hostage that cannot be exchanged. And it is this limit that terrorism reveals. As Baudrillard says: '[Terrorism] is not essentially political, but insists on identifying itself from the very first as the dream of a fantastic deal, the dream of an impossible exchange, and also as the denunciation of the impossibility of exchange' (*FS*, 50).

But if terrorism, a certain kind of terrorism, knows this, it is perhaps something that the social cannot take into account. That is, if in one way the social only arises because of a prior terrorism or the social pushed too far leads to terrorism, the social is only able to respond to this by an increased security, thus bringing about more terrorism. The social is only possible on the basis of the opposition it makes between itself and terrorism. Terrorism, by contrast, knows that ultimately it only lives on in exchange with the social; but it also knows that the social only lives on in exchange with it. And this is perhaps the real strategy at stake in its capturing of the hostage. For, by confronting the social with the problem of the inexchangeable, it actually forces it to exchange with it. Terrorism – through threatening the state with its own demise, the possibility that there will be no other with which it might exchange – is able to force the state to acquiesce to it, to concede to its demands. It knows that the state cannot entirely do away with terrorism, that terrorism is what justifies – and indeed allows – it. And terrorism perhaps even knows that it is not actually opposed to the state, but what arises at a certain point to save the state from itself. In a sense, that is, a little like the auction, it is through risking its own existence, proposing an exchange with the other without knowing whether anything will return, whether there is anyone to exchange with, that terrorism

initiates exchange – and, furthermore, exchange is always like
this; at the origin of exchange we can never be sure whether
there is anyone to exchange with or what is being exchanged. It
is by appearing not to follow the social that terrorism makes
the social follow it; it is by appearing not to take the social into
account that it accounts for it. Terrorism *seduces* the social. As
Baudrillard suggests of this necessary exchange or backing
down by the social, the way it is forced to save a terrorism that
appears indifferent to its own fate: '"What price will you pay to
be rid of terrorism?" Understood: terrorism is still a lesser evil
than a police state capable of ending it. It is possible that we
acquiesce in this fantastic proposition' (*FS*, 46; see also *CM I*,
190).

Finally, then, what relationship is there between terrorism –
and a terroristic theory like Baudrillard's – and this impossible
exchange? As we say, this 'beyond value' is not something it
could directly control or master. It is not something that could
be used by terrorism against the social, but exists only in the
very relationship between the two. That is, if in one way it
precedes terrorism as what allows it to enter into a relationship
with the social, in another way it comes about only after
terrorism, as an effect of its exchange with the social. This is
also why, if terrorism risks that the social will not exchange
with it and thereby wagers its demise, this risk also only arises
retrospectively, for insofar as terrorism exists at all it has
already been exchanged for the social. It is not so much a
matter of directly thinking something excluded as of thinking
what is excluded to ensure that things are exactly the way they
are, not so much a matter of directly thinking the inexchangeable as the *possibility* of exchange not taking place, for which
the social and terrorism both stand in. The failure of exchange
occurs *as* exchange. The following passage is not from *Fatal
Strategies* but from the earlier *In the Shadow*, but in it we can
see Baudrillard speaking of how terrorism would relate to this
outside that, like the hostage, is at once incomparable and
always compared, inexchangeable and always exchanged,
unrepresentable and always represented: the masses. But,
again, he stresses how terrorism would represent these masses

not straightforwardly but only obliquely, 'blindly' (*SSM*, 52);
how, if the masses precede terrorism, are what terrorism seeks
to express or speak for, they are also only after terrorism, an
effect of it. The relationship between terrorism and the masses,
therefore, is not that between two comparables, two represen-
tations, but – and here we return to that 'aristocratic parity' at
stake in the auction – between two incomparables that are
alike in their very difference, two things which in their exclusion allow themselves to be represented:

> Indeed, the only phenomenon which may be in a relationship
> of affinity with [this negativity], with these masses such that
> the final vicissitude of the social and its death is at stake, is
> terrorism. Nothing is more 'cut off' from the masses than
> terrorism. Power may very well try to set one against the
> other, but nothing is more strange, more familiar either, than
> their convergence in denying the social and refusing
> meaning. [. . .]
>
> Terrorism does not aim at making anything speak, at
> resuscitating or mobilizing anything; it has no revolutionary
> consequences (in this regard, it is rather a complete counter-
> performance); it aims at the masses in their silence, a silence
> mesmerized by information; it aims at that white magic of
> the social encircling us, that of information, of simulation,
> of deterrence, of anonymous and random control. It aims at
> that white magic of social abstraction by the black magic of
> a still greater, more anonymous, arbitrary and hazardous
> abstraction: that of the terrorist act.
>
> It is the only non-representative act. In this regard, it has
> an affinity with the masses, who are the only non-
> representable reality. This is definitely not to say that
> terrorism would *represent* the silence and the not-said of the
> masses; that it would violently express their passive
> resistance. It is simply to say: there is no equivalent to the
> blind, non-representative, senseless character of the terrorist
> act but the blind, senseless and unrepresentational
> behaviour of the masses. (*SSM*, 50, 51–2)

All this would apply, of course, to Baudrillard's own attempts
to represent terrorism, the hostage, the masses, the 'beyond
value' of exchange. He could not do so directly, but only as it
were indirectly, not by simulating the masses but by being

seduced by them. Thus – and this again against the obvious realist reading of his work – terrorism, the hostage, the masses, even exchange itself, only stand in for, are only exchanged for, something else: just that paradox of the sign we spoke about at the beginning of the book. Baudrillard's writing, that is, like the terrorism it speaks of, attempts to form a relationship with that with which it cannot form a relationship, attempts to describe something that at once is excluded to allow it to be represented and only exists after the attempt to do so. In a sense, therefore, it must seek to represent *nothing*. But the risk and the strategy of writing – as of terrorism itself – is that it is only by daring to represent nothing, to offer nothing in exchange for the appearances of the world, that the world necessarily recognizes itself in it, that we catch the world up, bring about an exchange with it. Like terrorism in its relationship with the masses, writing does not simply speak for a pre-existing state of things, but makes the world over in its image. How best to resemble a world and its systems that, as we see in *Fatal Strategies* and elsewhere, are already at an extreme, obey only their own law, refer exclusively to themselves? Only by an equally 'aristo-cratic' writing that similarly resembles itself, follows its own law, drives its own internal logic to extremes. The world would be forced to act, to see itself in this writing, because, like the social, it is only insofar as it is exchanged for another, insofar as it is represented by another. Henceforth, the world resembles itself, accounts for itself, is equal to itself, only across the unbridgeable distance of its writing.

* * *

In all three cases – the collection, the auction, terrorism – we can see how a certain notion of exchange lies at the origin of things. However, to the extent that exchange is at the origin of things, we cannot say what this origin is (every exchange at once stands in for and defers this impossible exchange; we can only say what this origin is by exchanging it for something else). But, if these systems are only possible because of this limit, there is a different relationship to it than in simulation.

They do not attempt to speak of it, as in the third order of simulacra, but acknowledge that they can never speak of it; they do not try to take it into account because they know it is what allows all taking into account. Thus, in the collection, the subjective pleasure in finding the next piece, in bringing it to a conclusion, comes from the risk that we cannot find the next piece, that the collection is over and we no longer have any involvement with it. In the auction, value arises from the calculation that there is still another bid to go before the final bid, while knowing that the other parties are also basing their calculations on this so that this final bid might come at any moment. In the taking of hostages, it is by risking that the hostage will not be exchanged that the terrorist ends up exchanging the hostage, but this situation cannot be mastered by terrorism because it is itself only possible as a result of this exchange with the social.

In each case – though we have perhaps taken it up in a slightly unusual manner – we have what Baudrillard calls *seduction*. In its simplest terms, it is the idea that the system only arises in an exchange with the other, that the fundamental rule of the world is reversibility. The system only arises on the basis of its relationship with the other, but the system pushed too far in its resemblance to this other begins to produce the opposite effects from those intended, begins to resemble the other less and less. It is very close to simulation, which in its most advanced state, as we have seen, also proposes the system on the basis of its relationship to a certain other, but simulation in the end always tries to name this other, master this limit. Seduction is not entirely different from this, but it is also the thinking of that other excluded to allow the other to be named, that limit left out to allow the limit to be overcome. In each of the systems above, for example, there is no simple opening up to the other, a direct representation of it, but rather a simultaneous attempt to take it into account and to take into account the fact that we cannot take it into account. Seduction, that is, attempts to take into account what cannot be taken into account, seeks to form an economy with the other. It is on the basis of this impossible relationship with the other that value itself is founded (and in all of this there is the closest analogy between seduction as opposed to simulation and what Derrida calls 'general' as opposed to 'restricted' economy, both sets of concepts intriguingly developed through a certain reading of Bataille).

This sense of reversibility and the limits to systematicity it imposes runs throughout Baudrillard's career, but it is perhaps in *Symbolic Exchange and Death* that it is theorized explicitly for the first time. That book, as we might remember from our Introduction, is in part a history and sociology of the place of death in Western society, from the dead time or labour implied in the modern industrial process in the chapter 'The End of Production' (*SE*, 6–50), through the self-punishment and discipline required in the new regime of health and fitness in the chapter 'The Body, or the Grave of Signs' (*SE*, 101–24), and on to the actual suppression or hiding of death in the funeral parlour or retirement home in the chapter 'Political Economy and Death' (*SE*, 125–94). In the book, using examples from anthropology and 'primitive' societies, Baudrillard attempts to argue for the centrality of death within human experience and to assert its reality against all efforts to deny or rationalize it. But, as we also said in our Introduction, if *Symbolic Exchange* marks the high point of Baudrillard's work as a sociologist, at the same time death only stands in for a more general anxiety or nothingness. That is, in that kind of 'double strategy' we looked at in Chapter 1, if Baudrillard is arguing for a certain death as opposed to life, 'death' also precedes the very relationship between them. 'Death' is the very confusion between death and life, the reversibility of one into the other, the fact that neither is possible without the other. Life as a principle of linear accumulation tries to distinguish between them, but death – death in the sense of cyclical return – shows that they are finally inseparable. In other words, perhaps surprisingly, for Baudrillard it is life that is forward-looking, teleological, and death that denies an end, reveals that all things turn around and become their contrary. It is life that reaches the end and death that is immortal, never-ending. It is death here, then, that does not so much oppose or come at the end of life as explain it and make it possible. It is life that arises within a wider cycle of death. We can, of course, never experience death as such but life is only possible because of, can only be understood through, death. Death – the impossible exchange between life and death – *doubles* life (*SE*, 133–40).[4]

Baudrillard examines this reversibility – a reversibility he explicitly associates with death – in a number of intellectual fields in *Symbolic Exchange*. In the chapter 'Political Economy and Death', he looks at Freud's discussion of the death-drive in his *Beyond the Pleasure Principle* and *Civilization and Its Discontents*, and more specifically the distinction he draws there between the two 'opposed' principles of Eros and Thanatos (*SE*, 149–54). In the same chapter, he looks at Mauss's account of the custom of potlatch in 'primitive' societies in his *The Gift* (*SE*, 134–5). In the final chapter, 'The Extermination of the Name of God', he looks at Saussure's investigation of the phenomenon of the substitutability of signs in his study of Roman poetry in his *Anagrams* (*SE*, 195–210). In each case here, Baudrillard discerns a strange ambivalence. Each thinker gets close to the discovery or acknowledgement of the fundamental reversibility of the world: the inseparability of life and death in Freud; of value and the destruction of value in Mauss; of sense and nonsense in Saussure. And yet, if each intuits this underlying key to the meaning of the world, he also represses it in his work: if Freud saw the inseparability of Eros and Thanatos, he insisted in the end on opposing them or seeing them as mere complementaries; if Mauss saw the inseparability of value and waste, he nevertheless (as with the economists of *Consumer Society*) went on to condemn this in the name of economic or structuralist rationality; if Saussure saw the inseparability of sense and nonsense in Roman poetry, he did not publish his findings for fear of the effect they would have on the putative science of semiology. But perhaps, more than this, we would say that it is not only this reversibility as the basis of the world that is first seen in their work, but this reversibility that makes their various discourses so uniquely powerful. In other words, in a paradox originally pointed out by Foucault in his essay 'What is an Author?', we would say that the defining quality of great thinkers, of the so-called 'initiators of discursive practices' (Foucault 1977b: 131), is that they somehow redis-cover or re-create in their work this fundamental reversibility of the world; but at the same time, in order to make this work a discipline, they must also attempt to systematize that which cannot be systematized. In a way, that reversibility they discover is both what makes their thought possible and that which cannot be thought. It is the ability to repeat or produce this reversal that is the mark of great writing, but this is precisely beyond the ability of any individual consciously to do so, or any attempt to bring it about would only have the effect of losing it. These authors themselves would only be the effect of it. This is why Baudrillard himself advocates a reversal of these figures in *Symbolic Exchange* – a 'turning of Mauss against Mauss, Saussure against Saussure and Freud against Freud' (*SE*, 1) – but also why this reversal could only take place in their name, only continue a process they have already begun. We will return to this in our Conclusion.

Seduction

It is in his book *Seduction* that Baudrillard first begins to explore this reversibility in a fully metaphysical way, under-standing the limitation it poses not only to those systems he examines but also to his own attempts to describe it. That is, if in *Symbolic Exchange* death can still be understood as real, provided with a concrete historical actuality, seduction is a much more nebulous topic, a creation in a sense of narratives and folklore (the archetypal stories and myths of seduction), operating entirely through language. If in *Symbolic Exchange* there is still a whole scholarly apparatus of proper names, footnotes, facts and dates, by the time of *Seduction* this has disappeared in a series of statements that apparently need no other authority than themselves. And in line with Baudrillard's new emphasis upon the creative power of language, *Seduction* is perhaps his most beautifully written book, the one where he first discovers his mature style. It is cool, lucid, not overtly poetic but imbued with great rhetorical charge. The tone is not directly polemical or argumentative, as *Symbolic Exchange* still is, but aloof, dispassionate, abstract, as though reciting a legend or fairytale. (If the image of theory in *In the Shadow* or *Fatal Strategies* is terrorism, in *Seduction* it is a kind of fiction or fable.) But this choice of tone is interesting. If a new power is accorded to language, if Baudrillard realizes that the theorist is no longer able to maintain an objective or scientific distance from his or her subject, this does not lead to an anarchic, 'libidinal' way of writing, as with similar efforts at the time (for example, Lyotard in his *Libidinal Economy* or Deleuze and Guattari in their *Anti-Oedipus*). On the contrary, for Baudrillard theory's strongest effects – we hope we have made this clear by now – arise not from a lack but from an *excess* of order, not from subjective desire but by following the objective tendencies of the world to their furthest extent. That is, Baudrillard, is not taking a distance from the processes he describes, not trying to *reflect* these in his prose style, as it could be argued Lyotard and Deleuze and Guattari do when they write in their deliberately fragmented, 'schizophrenic' manner. Rather, in the difficult distinction we are trying to draw out here, we would say that Baudrillard's writing *embodies* this disorder, does not try to master it or comment upon it but is subject to it, an effect of it. In speaking of the fundamental seduction of the world, it too wants to be seduced. It is to know that, insofar as what he is speaking of is true, he cannot say what it is, cannot directly imitate it. It is only by driving the inner logic of his writing to its furthest point, by it imitating nothing but itself, that he might somehow capture it, that this seduction might come about in writing or this writing be shown to be an effect of seduction.

So what then is this seduction that is the apparent object of Baudrillard's book? We said earlier it was the distance between things that allows their resemblance or the distance that arises when their resemblance is pushed too far. Or, as we saw when we looked at those examples a moment ago involving exchange, it is that void before things for which they stand in and through which they are exchanged – but a void that only comes about through the very attempt to stand in for it and exchange itself through it. And we see these two sides of seduction in the book. For example, towards the beginning of *Seduction* Baudrillard recounts the famous myth of Narcissus and Echo, that ancient Greek tale in which Narcissus mistakes a reflection of himself for another and ends up pining away, commemorated only by Echo's voice. However, as opposed to the usual interpretations of the tale which emphasize the role either of Narcissus or Echo, for Baudrillard the crucial protagonist is precisely the surface of the water in its role as a mirror. But if it is the role of the water Baudrillard stresses as against those other readings, it is nevertheless not the key to or explanation of the myth. Why? Because the mirror, if it allows the essential confusion of Narcissus' reflection with another's, cannot itself be represented. Any attempt to do so, to give the mirror an image, only as it were stands in for it, sees a reflection of itself in it. As Baudrillard says of the mirror as a figure for seduction in the story: 'Seduction cannot possibly be represented because in seduction the distance between the real and its double, the same and the other, is abolished' (*S*, 67).[5] However, if we can add anything to Baudrillard's formulation here, we would say that we cannot represent seduction, that seduction is always lost in any description of it, because seduction *is* this distance between the real and its double, the same and the other, which allows the distinction between them to be abolished in this way. Seduction cannot be represented because seduction is always being represented, because seduction is representation itself.

We see this also in another defining tale of seduction Baudrillard offers towards the beginning of the book. It is the story of the little boy who is granted any wish he wants by a genie so long as he does not think of the red of a fox's tail. Of course, no sooner does the genie say this than the boy is consumed by this image of the red of the fox's tail, spends the rest of his life obsessed by it and eventually goes mad. But perhaps the point here is not so much that the boy actually spends his time thinking about the fox's tail. Rather, it is that, after the genie's command – and this in a way like those other examples we gave above concerning exchange – everything the boy does, even not thinking of the red of a fox's tail, is only to stand in for it, take its place, is exactly *not* to think of the red of a fox's tail (*S*, 74–5). (And we cannot but suspect here that this fox's tail is only to stand in for something else, that for which everything stands in: representation itself.) We see something similar in another tale Baudrillard relates concerning seduction, the famous anecdote 'Death in Samarkand', from Somerset Maugham's play *Sheppey*. It is a story about a man who one day accidentally comes upon Death at a crossroads. The man, fearful for his life, runs in the opposite direction and travels all that day and into the next night to arrive finally, exhausted and out of breath, at the last place he thinks Death would look for him, the obscure town of Samarkand. Meanwhile, the King has summoned Death to his court, where he reprimands him for scaring one of his subjects. Death replies that he had not meant to do so but was surprised to see him there as he already had an appointment with him the next night in Samarkand (*S*, 72–4)! Here too the point is not so much that Death as a figure is anywhere in particular as that he is that for which everything stands in, underlies all of our actions, is present even in his absence. Indeed, in a way as with the genie, we cannot even say that Death is that which precedes us and that towards which we run, but rather must say that Death does not exist before us, is only an effect of our attempting to run away from him. It is our very attempt to escape fate that is our fate. The truth of Death's prediction is not fulfilled until we try to refute it. We spend the whole of our lives trying to avoid the fate which becomes in retrospect the very fate we always had.[6]

It is this uncanny power that Baudrillard wants to invest his own discourse with. It is not that it actually predicts or determines anything; the world can run anywhere it wants – but this only to play out its prediction, only as a fulfilment of its decree. That is, Baudrillard's work does not so much add anything to the world or change anything about it as *subtract* something from it: after it, the world just as it is can only be explained because of it. The very reality of the world, its ability to account for itself, is only possible in and through the void it opens up, only as it were by standing in for it, taking its place. This is why seduction – Baudrillard's thinking of seduction – is not simply opposed to simulation, but is what allows and disallows it, enables it to become infinite but only because of what it excludes. Take, for instance, Baudrillard's arguments concerning pornography, and more particularly the so-called 'vaginal cyclorama' by means of which 'Japanese workers in their shirt-sleeves (it is a popular spectacle) are permitted to shove their noses up to their eyeballs within the woman's vagina in order to see, to see better' (*S*, 31). Where is the seduction in this? Exactly nowhere. Both are cases where there is an attempt to strip away all seduction, all ritual, all distance in order to see the 'thing itself'. And yet at the same time we suspect that the very effort to do so only arises on the basis of a fundamental fear that something is missing, that the thing we are looking for is not there. It is this that provokes the endless investigation into women's genitals; but it is also this that ensures that there is always further to go, that its hyper-visibility is haunted by the fear of blindness, something that cannot be seen. As Baudrillard says:

> If the obscene is a matter of representation and not of sex, it must explore the very interior of the body and the viscera. Who knows what profound pleasure is to be found in the visual dismemberment of mucous membranes and smooth muscles? Our pornography still retains a restricted definition. Obscenity has an unlimited future. (*S*, 32)

That is to say, again, seduction can never be entirely done away with because the very attempt to do so can only be undertaken on its basis. Even in the most explicit sexual proposition, the most violent attempt to traverse the distance separating the same and the other, there is always a kind of ambiguity or distance. It is always possible that our words remain unclear (even to ourselves), that the other does not understand by them the same thing we do. And, inversely, even in the other's acceptance of our invitation, it is possible that this is not what it appears, that another motivation lies behind it (the desire to seduce someone else, for example). But it is this ambiguity that allows sexual seduction to occur in the first place. The two parties simply wouldn't come together if there was not some distance separating them; or if there was no such distance they would soon break up, lose interest in each other. As Baudrillard explains, citing a passage from the science-fiction novelist Philip K. Dick's *The Schizophrenic's Ball*:

> 'Take me to your room and fuck me.'
> 'There is something indefinable in your vocabulary, something yet to be desired.'
> One can understand this as: your proposition is unaccept-able, it lacks the poetry of desire, it is too direct. But in a sense the text says the exact opposite: that the proposition has something 'indefinable' about it, which thereby *opens* the path to desire. A direct sexual invitation is too direct to be true, and immediately refers to something else. [. . .] In the last instance, a purely sexual statement, a pure demand for sex, is impossible. One cannot be free of seduction, and the discourse of anti-seduction is but its last metamorphosis. (*S*, 42–3)

It is in this sense that we must understand the last chapter of *Seduction*, 'The Political Destiny of Seduction'. Baudrillard raises there – as the reverse side of the great narratives of seduction from a now by-gone aristocratic age he discusses – the question of the future of seduction, the possibility that it is only a thing of the past, only to be seen in an always simulated form. That is, he traces the passage of seduction from the 'dual, antagonistic' play of the 'rule' through the 'statutory polarity' of the 'law' and finally to the 'ludic digitality' of the 'norm' (*S*, 155–6). We no longer have the real space and otherness of seduction, but only – as in the third order of simulacra – a distance projected by the system itself, in which as in the poll the answer is already implicit in the question, the question only able to be asked in light of the answer: 'Seduce me' or 'Let me seduce you' (*S*, 175). It is a bit like that world of endless care, incessant solicitation, conjured up at the end of *Consumer Society*, in which all anxieties are 'seduced' away, in which we are allowed to be seduced, to seduce others, but only within absolutely defined parameters (the new rules of social intercourse). Baudrillard writes:

> Seduction suggests the workings of a social world that we no longer comprehend, and a political world whose structures have faded. In the place of the latter, seduction gives rise to an immense blank area traversed by tepid currents of speech, or a malleable network lubricated by magnetic impulses. The world is no longer driven by power but fascination, no longer by production but seduction. This seduction is, however, no more than an empty declaration formed of simulated concepts. The discourses held by both the 'strategists' of mass desire (the politicians, advertisers, organizers, engineers of the soul, and of the mind, etc.) and the 'analysts' of their strategies, these discourses that describe the functioning of the social or the political, or what remains of them, in terms of seduction, they are as vacuous as the political space itself. (*S*, 173–4)

This, indeed, is the question Baudrillard leaves us with at the end of *Seduction*. Which is it to be: is this simulation to be seduction's 'destiny' or 'can we oppose this involutional fate and lay a wager on seduction as destiny' (*S*, 180)? But, as we saw in *The Transparency of Evil*, and against Baudrillard here, there is in fact no choice. If seduction is always being simulated, no sooner represented than a copy, this itself, as Baudrillard himself says, is only because of seduction, is only to lead to a new form of seduction. We might only have simulation, the forward march of simulation, but this only as the attempt to do away with seduction, only in response to a prior seduction. The absence of seduction can only be explained because of seduction itself, which is why Baudrillard emphasizes that seduction – as the very myths through which it appears – is immortal, archetypal, an essential 'form' to the world. Before seduction ends and simulation becomes total, seduction itself intervenes, simulation is led astray to some other end or purpose. The very totality of simulation now means something else, is able to be seen as suggesting some other fate than its own, heading in a direction it does not foresee, having to be explained for a completely other reason than the one it provides.

'Diary of the Seducer'

But to end this chapter, we might give two examples of this seductive strategy in operation, how this play with and within limits takes place in everyday life. Our first example is Baudrillard's discussion of Kierkegaard's 'Diary of the Seducer' in *Seduction*. As we say, *Seduction* is in part a meditation upon the long history of seduction in music and literature, music and literature as themselves seductive. It both wants to belong to this tradition – while re-inventing certain effects within it – and is an elegy, whether mistaken or not, for the end of this tradition. And Baudrillard sees Kierkegaard's essay 'Diary of the Seducer', part of his much longer work *Either/Or*, as itself both the high point of this tradition and perhaps its last great instance (just as Kierkegaard himself in his book looks at arguably the first great instance of seduction in the modern sense, Mozart's *Don Giovanni*). 'Diary of the Seducer' is a fictionalized account, in journal form, of the character Johannes's attempts to seduce the young girl Cordelia, loosely based on events from Kierkegaard's own life when he left his fiancée Regine Olsen in controversial circumstances. In Kierkegaard's book, it is part of the wider shift from the aesthetic to the ethical and ultimately the religious, but that is not Baudrillard's concern here. Though in the end Kierkegaard rejects Johannes's act of seduction, thinking he can master the paradoxes it poses through an even more paradoxical exercise of faith, for Baudrillard seduction – and this even to go against that earlier prognosis of its decline – is impossible to go beyond: the ethical, the religious, non-seduction, are only themselves the last of seduction's own strategies (*S*, 115). And yet at the same time Baudrillard opens up the possibility of a certain reversal of Johannes's strategy that might be the equivalent to Kierkegaard's religious. That is, he will show against Johannes that there is no final strategy of seduction, no way of mastering it or saying what it is – and this might be the earthly match of Kierkegaard's paradoxical faith in God.

What happens in 'Diary of the Seducer'? Johannes in his account is a middle-aged man, tired with the world, for whom life has lost its novelty and allure. Perhaps as a last attempt to revive his interest in things, he sets about to seduce the beautiful virgin Cordelia, about whom a young man comes to see him for advice. Under the guise of helping him by acting as his intermediary, Johannes insinuates himself into her family, ingratiates himself with her mother. Cordelia herself becomes conscious of him, although at no point does he ever directly approach her or suggest any liaison. Gradually, her affections change object. Such is Johannes's charm that she decides to break off her relationship with the younger man and become engaged to Johannes. At this point, his task is accomplished, his seduction of her complete. He no longer has any need of the girl and cancels the proposed union. Of course, in those days – as Kierkegaard well knew – such an action cast a terrible slur upon the woman, implying perhaps that she was no longer intact or was otherwise unfit for marriage. Cordelia, although nothing has actually happened to her – there is certainly no sexual relationship between the two – is now a broken woman, unable to return to the young man who loved her (and whom, she realizes too late, she also loved) and rejected by a man towards whom she has no feelings.

This is the bare outline of the action of 'Diary of the Seducer', but the main interest of the text concerns Johannes's strategy for seducing Cordelia, for winning her away from her intended and making her his own. How does he do this? It is not as though there are any obvious physical attractions or attributes he possesses. He is a mature man, not especially wealthy, and she is young, beautiful and untouched. Rather, his strategy is to become her 'mirror' (*S*, 43). (The story takes place – here we might think back to the beginning of *The System of Objects* – in closed, bourgeois interiors, full of polished furniture and shining surfaces.) As Baudrillard says of Johannes's strategy, citing Kierkegaard: 'A mirror hangs on the opposite wall; she does not reflect on it, but the mirror reflects her' (*S*, 105).

Through his contact with Cordelia's family, he aims to become indispensable to her. Without him representing anything in particular – for he does not want anything from her, acts only under the pretext of another – she becomes conscious of him. Indeed, precisely because he is not distinctive, is not memorable, she cannot exactly recall when or how she first became conscious of him. When she does become conscious of him, therefore, she also becomes conscious of the fact that she is conscious of him: he is 'interesting in the second degree' (*S*, 117). She becomes, perhaps for the first time in her young life, self-conscious, reflective. And conscious, first of all, that she is only aware of herself through another. She thus realizes that her identity does not stand apart, inviolate, but comes about only through reflection, comparison, exchange – which, as we have been trying to say, means that she only knows of herself as another, in relation to another. She becomes aware that the world is represented or comes about only through representation. In a word, she is seduced. Her life as it once was – and without appearing to be touched on the surface – is now only possible for a completely different reason: only insofar as it is reflected in another, only insofar as another reflects her. She needs this other as each of us needs our own reflection, and this is undoubtedly why she ends up wanting to marry Johannes.

We might put this another way. In one sense, Cordelia becomes conscious of Johannes, but in another sense it is not he she is conscious of but herself. The reason why he is intriguing to her – even though he is nothing – is because it is he who allows her to become conscious of herself. And this is why she can never get to the bottom of him: because he – like the mirror of Narcissus – is what precedes and makes her possible. No matter how much she reflects on him, and reflects upon herself reflecting upon him, she can never completely understand him, is never able to say when she first became aware of him, because he is what precedes and allows this reflection. He is a kind of absence within her, a nothing around which she is formed. And yet at the same time, we would say that, if she does not exist before he reflects her for herself, if she arises only in response to his reflection, he is also only arbitrary, a reflection of or arising in response to some innate predisposition (S, 100). He only stands in for a kind of void already within her and which comes about as a result of her efforts to represent herself to herself. (And this is perhaps in the end what Kierkegaard means by speaking of Johannes as 'interesting in the second degree': that ultimately she is unable to decide whether it is her consciousness of him which allows her to become self-conscious or her own self-consciousness which makes her conscious of him.)

This is the risk of the seducer's strategy. Johannes is able to reflect Cordelia, force her to become conscious of herself, open up an abyss within her; but he also knows that all this is only to respond to something within her, that he must await her becoming conscious of him, that he only stands in for a process already underway. He can destine or double Cordelia – so that her own self-consciousness, her lack of awareness of him, is only possible because of him, is only deliberately *not* to think of him – but only after she becomes self-conscious. That is, the risk Johannes takes is that Cordelia *is* self-conscious. For, again – and this is the point of seduction as Baudrillard intends it, why it is not to be mistaken for mere physical rape or defilement – nothing actually happens here, there is no proof anything takes place. Johannes never actually sleeps with or marries Cordelia, and ideally even the engagement and its breaking-off are unnecessary. The 'perfection' (S, 100) of his crime lies in the fact that she can never be sure it happened, cannot be certain whether it was he who robbed her of her self-identity or unconsciousness or whether it is this pre-existing loss which is merely reflected in him. It is this doubling without evidence that is the real seduction (S, 118). But, of course – and the question is whether he is aware of it or not – this opens up the possibility that the whole thing is in fact imagined by Johannes, that Cordelia is truly unconscious, that her apparent unself-consciousness and obliviousness of him is not feigned but real. That is, the whole scenario can be reversed and it is Cordelia who can be seen to allow Johannes to become aware of himself, who makes Johannes self-conscious. This is the meaning of 'Diary of the Seducer''s confessional, diary-like form: it is possible that as we read it nothing of this actually occurred, that its only reality is in the imagination of Johannes. And this question applies as well to Baudrillard's own reading of the text (and to ours here as well).

This is the risk seduction runs: that the world, which we see as following our hypothesis even in its very indifference to it, is in fact truly indifferent. And this risk is the same, strangely enough, as saying that it only feigns indifference, that it seduces us. (This is why Baudrillard can say that Cordelia's virginity constitutes a challenge to Johannes, that Johannes in fact is only responding to a prior seduction.) In other words, the ultimate aim of seduction is to ensure that the other cannot remain indifferent, that their apparent indifference or unself-conscious-ness can only be explained because of us; and yet at the same time it is always possible that the other is only feigning indifference, that our belief that we are destining the other is only their destining of us. And, in a sense, it is just this that we are constantly seeking to take into account. The very possibility of winning the game – ensuring that the other is not indifferent – also opens up the possibility that we might lose – that the other's apparent indifference is only feigned. At every step we try to take this indifference of the other into account, but it is just this that opens up the possibility of another move after us, a deliberate conformity to *this*. And this is the true strategy of seduction, as we have seen in the collection, the auction and terrorism: we must at once try to stand in for the relationship between the same and the other; but we also know that this relationship comes about only after our attempt to stand in for it, that this attempt to stand in for it also opens up the possibility of another coming after us. We only seduce insofar as we risk being seduced; we only seduce insofar as we cannot know whether we seduce or are seduced. This is perhaps the secret to that famous irony in Kierkegaard, the distance he takes from his various narrators (his pseudonymous authorships, his use of framing fictional devices, his adoption of a narrative 'voice' that appears to undercut what is being said, etc.): Johannes might think that he masters seduction, is in control of Cordelia, but we can see that, despite himself, it is he in the end who is seduced.

'Please Follow Me'

The second example of seduction we look at here is Baudrillard's essay on the French Conceptual artist Sophie Calle, 'Please Follow Me'. It concerns a work by Calle, the so-called *Venetian Suite*, in which, having met a man at a party in Paris and found out that he is going on a trip to Venice alone, Calle decides to go there herself and follow him without his knowing. She takes photos of him and keeps a diary of her activities as she tracks him around, which are finally presented as the finished work of art. But what is the purpose of Calle's activity? What is she trying to say by means of her work? At first sight, she simply appears to be spying on him, trying to find out whether he has any secrets, what he gets up to when he is alone, whether he leads a double life. But Baudrillard rejects or complicates this likely hypothesis, which for him is too obvious, too subjective:

> It serves no purpose to discover by shadowing someone that he has a double life, except to heighten curiosity for instance – the important point is that it is *the shadowing itself which is the other's double life*. To shadow the other is *de facto* to give him a double life, a parallel existence. ('FM', 104)

In other words, it is not simply that Calle by her shadowing wants to discover a secret about the man, but that by this means she in fact imbues his life with a secret, a hidden destiny, it did not have before. That is, merely by following him and appearing to obey his every wish – and here we might think back to Johannes's strategy *vis-à-vis* Cordelia – she as it were destines him, denies him his free will, makes everything he does seem as though it was done for an entirely different reason than the one he gives himself. By following him, she makes it seem as though he is in a sense following her. Or, at least, it becomes impossible to say whether she is following him or he is following her, who is imitating whom. As Baudrillard says, if in one way he on his own free time seems to be able to do just what he wants to, in another way 'it is as if someone, behind him, knew he was going nowhere' ('FM', 103).

But, more than this, Calle's intention is that the man some-how feel this, become aware he is being followed. Even though she does nothing to draw his attention to her, even though there is no evidence for it – for Calle hopes not to be dis-covered by the man, when the game would simply be over – the man can perhaps feel this loss of will within himself, sense himself giving way to some other destiny. It is only in this manner that Calle can win the game with the man, insofar as he actually knows he is being seduced, insofar as his apparent indifference is not genuine. And yet at the same time, as with Johannes and Cordelia, Calle would not begin to follow the man unless she was in a way seduced by him, convinced – despite what Baudrillard says above – that he does indeed have a secret life. Here, of course, it is the man who leads her and she who follows the man. It is she who puts herself in his hands, who passes out of herself, via the medium of the man. Her day-to-day cares, her normal responsibilities, even the apparent essentials of life – all become insignificant in relation to the apparently ineluctable necessity of following the man. As Baudrillard writes (and, as he points out, this would apply equally to Johannes in 'Diary of the Seducer'):

> You are seduced by being absent, by simply being the mirror of the other who does not know it – just like that of Kierkegaard, suspended on the opposite wall: the young girl is unaware of it, but the mirror knows. You are seduced by being the destiny of the other, the double of his course which, for him, has a meaning, but which, redoubled, hasn't anymore. ('FM', 103)

There is thus a game, a duel, set up: who is seducing whom? Is it Calle who seduces the man or the man who seduces Calle? Is it she who gives meaning to his life or he who gives meaning to hers? Who is following whom? And what we see – as in all questions of seduction – is that neither alternative is possible without the other, neither the man's activity nor Calle's follow-ing is possible before the exchange of each for the other. The man's secret or destiny (even for himself) does not exist before he is seduced by Calle's shadowing, and Calle's shadowing would not be undertaken before she was seduced by the man.

And Baudrillard expresses this mutual reciprocity – which is a 'gift' ('FM', 107) for both, produces something out of nothing – very well. He writes:

> Did she at bottom want him to kill her, or, finding this shadowing unbearable (especially since she anticipated nothing, least of all a sexual adventure), to hurl himself upon her to do violence to her – or looking back at her like Orpheus leading Eurydice from the Underworld, to make her suddenly disappear? Did she simply want to be his destiny, or for him to become her own destiny? As in every game, this had its fundamental rule: nothing must come of it, no event which might form a contact or relationship between them. Such is the price of seduction. The secret must not be broken, on pain of falling back into a banal history.
>
> Of course, there is something murderous for the one who is followed. He can take offence and fall back into persecution. But that is not Sophie's aim (even if the phantasm of awakening it was present the whole time – but she also runs a risk: the other, having detected the stratagem, can turn the situation around and submit her to any fate he chooses – he is not a victim, basically his power is as great as hers). ('FM', 104)

But it is at this point that we can see the real stakes of seduction opened up: that the man, 'having detected the stratagem, can turn the situation around and submit her to any fate he chooses'. For, having discovered that he is being followed by Calle – and, remember, she cannot attempt to win the game without him being aware of it – it is not in turning around and telling her he knows that he might triumph or get his own back. In that case, the game simply comes to an end and his triumph would be short-lived. Rather, as Baudrillard suggests, his best attempt to win the game would be to feign ignorance of the fact that he is being followed and let her believe she is still following him. She would be wasting her time and he would truly be leading her. And all this, as we say, because Calle for her part cannot simply let the man know she has been following him. Here too the game would be short-lived. That is, neither party can attempt to win the game directly but only indirectly, only by opening up the possibility of losing. From Calle's side, she can attempt to win by not letting the man know he is being followed only to open up the possibility both that he is simply not aware of being followed and that he is aware he is being followed and is in fact leading her. From the man's side, he can attempt to win by feigning ignorance that he is being followed only to open up the possibility both that Calle is not following him and that Calle knows he knows and has somehow taken this into account. But then Calle's taking of this into account opens up the possibility of him taking *this* into account, and so on. There is a kind of asymptotic process of taking into account each other's strategy – Calle follows, the man knows Calle follows, Calle knows the man knows Calle follows . . . – that is the real game of seduction here and which in a way we have been trying to describe throughout this chapter. It is this, for example, that we saw in the auction and it is this which accounts for that 'fitful, halting' rhythm we see both there and here, which Baudrillard describes as 'not too fast, not too slow' ('FM', 108).[7] For we can imagine the two parties moving along the streets of Venice, like the two bidders in an auction, at once wanting to finish their calculations before moving, not wanting to move for fear of being discovered and allowing the other to take them into account, and having to move, to continue either following or leading in an attempt to win the game. Each is at once *too soon*, because it is possible that the other is indifferent, because the other can always take his or her strategy into account, and *too late*, because there is no indifference within the game, because the other is always able to see him or her as enacting a strategy, because each is able to act only insofar as he or she is already in a relationship with the other.

What then is the final aim of seduction? What is the real point of the various parties' followings and their attempts to take into account the possibility that they are being followed, etc? It is ultimately to make the indifference of the other impossible, to rule out the possibility that he or she is not playing the game. As Baudrillard suggests, the whole purpose of Calle's following is not in the end to find out or induce secrets about the man, or even really to win the game. It is rather to make it seem as though his indifference, his possible unawareness of the game, is only feigned, a strategy, as though, 'having detected the stratagem, [he] can turn the situation around and submit her to any fate he chooses'. And what is the reason for the man's going around Venice without looking back? Only to keep open the possibility that he is being followed, that the other's absence is only a deliberate strategy on her part in order to win the game. In fact, it is possible that, just as the man is unaware of Calle, so Calle is unaware of the man. But both by a kind of doubling hypothesis attempt to exclude this possibility. The indifference of the man is now only proof he is aware of her strategy and a deliberate refusal to look back. The absence of Calle is now only proof she is following him. But at the same time, if each is able to determine the behaviour of the other in this way, this also opens up the possibility that the other is only conforming to this strategy: that the man is only *pretending* to be indifferent; that Sophie is *aware* the man knows he is being followed. And we might say that each twist in their respective strategies, each reversal in who follows and who is followed, attempts to exorcize this fundamental indifference, to make it seem as though this indifference is only a still more sophisticated attempt to win the game.[8] Each of these doublings is intended to show that the identity with the world formed by the one before is only to be explained for another reason, because of a conformity that separates them. To the doubling of the one before, each proposes a certain counter-doubling. It is not directly to oppose them, but by following them to their furthest reach to show that they are possible only for another reason, that their identity to the world is only guaranteed by the difference between them and the world, by the will of another. If we have attempted to show that each of the figures Baudrillard discusses – the collector, the bidder, the terrorist, the seducer – is a figure for the analyst, Calle is also a figure for him. Like Calle, by following the systems he analyses, Baudrillard wants to show how they are in fact following him or that it is impossible to say who is following whom, which is fine for him but fatal for these systems, which can only understand themselves as pure, closed off from the other, or at least ideally so (*PC*, 151). The aim of theory is not to win the game, but to overcome the indifference of the world or to oppose to the indifference of the world an even greater indifference. But to see all this in more detail, we turn now to our third and final chapter.

Notes

1. For two of the better attempts to address Baudrillard's relationship to feminism, see Sadie Plant, 'Baudrillard's Woman: The Eve of Seduction' (1993) and A. Keith Goshorn, 'Valorizing "the Feminine" While Rejecting Feminism? – Baudrillard's Feminist Provocations' (1994).

2. Genosko says that we can name symbolic exchange only by 'effraction' (1994: 11), that it is a kind of 'non-place' (1994: 16); but it is also always named, only somewhere within the four fractions of the following formula:

$$\frac{\text{EcEV}}{\text{UV}} = \frac{\text{Sr}}{\text{Sd}} \left(\frac{\text{Economic Exchange Value}}{\text{Use Value}} = \frac{\text{Signifier}}{\text{Signified}} \right);$$

in other words, symbolic exchange at once allows and disallows their 'convertibility' (1994: 6). For a review bringing out the 'double bind' of Baudrillard's activity, the limit to his ability to name this outside to economic exchange, see Joseph Valente, 'Hall of Mirrors: Baudrillard on Marx' (1985).

3. However, Baudrillard explores the emerging paradox of the modern work of art becoming both priceless and worthless in the current art boom, resembling that 'absolute merchandise' Charles Baudelaire once spoke of, in 'Beyond the Vanishing Point of Art' (1988b).

4. *Symbolic Exchange* is the book of Baudrillard's most obviously indebted to Derrida's deconstruction. Death, we would say, is the *différance* between life and death. Derrida himself speaks of this in such texts as 'Living On: Border Lines' and *The Gift of Death* (and Baudrillard's whole notion of symbolic exchange could be compared in detail to Derrida's concept of the 'gift').

5. It is interesting to note that French feminist philosopher Luce Irigaray plays on the relationship between woman and the mirror in her *Speculum of the Other Woman*, and on woman as at once infinitely exchanged and inexchangeable in the essays 'Women on the Market' and 'Commodities Among Themselves' in her *This Sex Which is Not One*. Irigaray has in fact responded positively to Baudrillard's writings on seduction in 'Woman is Nothing and That is Her Power' (1980).

6. See on this 'self-fulfilling (or self-defeating)' quality of seduction (*S*, 75). Baudrillard will also use the example of Borges's famous story 'The Lottery of Babylon', where things just as they are are doubled by the assumption of a certain fate (*S*, 150–3). Another Borges story that might be considered in these terms is 'The Zahir' (1981: 189–202), where a coin precisely seduces or doubles

a man's life, so that even not to think of it is to think of it (and to think of it is in a way not to think of it). Importantly, money as we know also plays the role of the medium of exchange. Finally, in the chapter 'The Fatal, or, Reversible Imminence' (*FS*, 144–64), Baudrillard explores the hypothesis not that fate is opposed to chance but that fate makes chance possible. All this is undoubtedly very close to Nietzsche's conception of the Eternal Return.

7. We return here to the complex question of rhythm in the collection, the auction and seduction in general (*S*, 81, 110). In terms of this 'judgement' involved in seduction, the simultaneous necessity and impossibility of taking a meta-position with regard to it, we might consider Samuel Weber's remarks concerning Lyotard's efforts to construct a 'justice without criteria' in his 'Afterword' to Lyotard's *Just Gaming* (1985).

8. We might say that every move in the game attempts to take the conformity (difference) of the other into account, but this only because of a prior conformity, this only to open up the possibility of another conformity. In other words, the final structure of the game is the infinite overdetermination of the same basic alternative: either Calle follows the man or the man 'follows' Calle. There are any number of ways of arriving at this, but in the end we are always confronted with the same choice. In this sense, the highest strategy comes increasingly to resemble chance. We might compare all this to the game of 'odds-and-evens' in Edgar Allen Poe's 'The Purloined Letter', where also 'symbolic determination is not opposed to chance', but is 'what emerges as the syntax of chance' (Johnson 1977: 504). And this is perhaps what Baudrillard means by speaking of seduction as 'transfinite' (*S*, 134): not only that the beginning and the end are at once the same and infinitely different as in the collection and the auction, but also that the same situation (the world) can be doubled and redoubled indefinitely.

3

Doubling

In the two previous chapters we looked at the relationship between simulation and seduction in terms of a certain logic of representation. We spoke of the way that, if simulation goes too far in attempting to overcome the distance between the copy and original, seduction is both that distance which allows their resemblance and that distance which arises when their resemblance is too close. In this sense, seduction is neither simply opposed to simulation nor the same as it. Rather, it makes simulation at the same time possible and impossible. It is seduction as that necessary distance between things that calls up the infinite efforts of simulation to cross it, and it is seduction that means simulation is never complete. Seduction *doubles* simulation: though it can never be seen as such, can only ever be represented in simulated form, it is seduction that explains simulation. This is why Baudrillard is able to say that seduction is 'inextricable', 'inescapable', an essential form of the world. Seduction is unable to be destroyed or surpassed, not because it is anything, remains unchanged, but because this very destruction or surpassing can only take place by means of it, is what seduction is.

We see this in Baudrillard's attempts to *seduce* the various systems of simulation he analyses. He does not attempt directly to criticize them, name some limit to them in the real. As we found in Chapter 1, any such limit is only possible because of these systems, only leads to a further extension of them. (These systems of simulation propose their own doubling, so that, if we never have them as such, what is outside or other to them – Indians in the rainforest for anthropology or unspoilt nature for industrial production – only functions as evidence for them.) On the contrary, he wants to show that they are possible only for a completely different reason than the one they give themselves, that they must be explained altogether otherwise. It is to argue that their supposed match with the world, their ability to make the world over in their image, comes about because of a prior difference between them and the world, because of something they leave out from it. It is not simply to speak of an other to these systems of simulation, but to think that 'other' which ensures they have no other, that 'other' which is produced when they have no other. And the aim of theory for Baudrillard is to devise a statement about a system that at once follows its internal logic to the end, adds nothing to it, and inverts it entirely, reveals that it is not possible without this 'nothing'. It is a statement that is at once a pure *description* of the system, speaking of it in terms of the real, and a pure *prescription* of the system, demonstrating that it excludes the real. It is a statement that is at once totally specific to each system examined, having to be invented afresh each time, and absolutely universal, testifying to the fundamental reversibility that lies at the origin of the world. In *Consumer Society*, it is that the endless solicitation of the social is only possible because of anguish. In *In the Shadow*, it is that the social is only possible because of the masses. In *The System of Objects*, it is that the collection is only able to be completed insofar as the last piece is missing from it. In 'The Art Auction', it is that the object only has value insofar as it can be exchanged for something else. In 'The Hostage', it is that the security of the social is only possible insofar as terrorism remains. In 'Diary of the Seducer', it is that the innocence of Cordelia is only possible because it is reflected by Johannes. In 'Please Follow Me', it is that the free will of the man is only possible insofar as he is followed by Calle and that Calle is only able to follow the man insofar as he lets her.

In each case here, the object Baudrillard speaks of – anguish, the masses, the last piece of the collection, exchange, seduction – is at once particular to the system he examines and only stands in for that fundamental difference which allows all representation. It is both real, actually excluded from the system, and virtual, the very thing that means nothing is excluded from the system. And this again is the complex position of Baudrillard himself, at once outside and inside these systems of simulation. He must both criticize them, speak against them in the name of something real, and double them, argue in the name of something that does not yet exist. He must both represent something and know that it cannot be represented. It is precisely the complexity of this 'double strategy' that we see neither in Kellner's condemnation of Baudrillard for shifting from the 'critique' (1989: 13) of Marxism to the 'carnival' (1989: 93) of the postmodern nor in Levin's celebration of the 'metaphysical' (1996: 14) and 'satirical' (1996: 15) turn in his reasoning. What Kellner does not understand is that the central problem of Baudrillard's work is how to contest simulation when there is no outside standard by which to judge it, when we can no longer speak, as in Marxism, of some authentic human essence that is alienated or some true value of the workers' labour that is exploited. And, inversely, what Levin does not understand is that, even at his most abstract, Baudrillard is still trying to represent the real, responding to a world he sees as extreme, resembling nothing, with a theory that is similarly extreme, that resembles nothing. As Baudrillard says in his interview with Lotringer:

> You will ask me, why [theorists] are going to these extremes, if you don't suppose that at some point the world, and the universe too, is in the grips of a movement to extremes. There you are, apparently, forced to make an almost objective, rational hypothesis. It is impossible to think that theory can be nothing more than fiction. Otherwise no one would bother producing theory any more. You have to believe that going somewhere is not just a metaphor. And then, if it is a challenge, in any case there is a partner. It is no longer a dialectic,

but there is a rule of the game. Somewhere there must be a
limit that constitutes the real in order for there to be theory. A
point where things can stick, or from which they can take off.
(*BL*, 115–16)

This, finally, is what Kellner and Levin do not grasp about
Baudrillard's writing: the fact that it is neither an empirical
refutation of these systems of simulation which shares the
same real as them, nor a pure fiction which bears no relationship to them. Rather, the defining quality of Baudrillard's work
is that it is *both*. It is both an account of a world that is already
at an extreme, about which theory can say nothing, and a
driving of the world to this extreme, the taking of an only
implicit tendency within it and pushing it to its limit. It both
acknowledges that there is nothing to say about the world, that
this world can be exchanged for nothing else, and attempts to
show that the world would not be like this before its exchange
with theory. It is for this reason that writing can go to the end
of its logic, knowing that at some point the world must step in
and begin to resemble it. But this is also to say – this is why
not just any discourse will do – that writing is only able to go
to this extreme because it follows the immanent order of the
world. This is what writing or theory *doubling* the world
means. It only repeats the world and the world does not exist
before this repetition. It only stands in for the difference
between the world and itself and this difference cannot be seen
before it. The world lacks nothing before its writing, but, after
it, can only be explained on its basis. It is a 'nothing' which
theory both makes visible and takes the place of, reveals and
covers over. It is a 'nothing' which both is and, insofar as it is at
all, cannot be (*PC*, 1). As Baudrillard says in the chapter
'Radical Thought' of *The Perfect Crime*:

Radical thought is at the violent intersection of meaning and
non-meaning, of truth and non-truth, of the continuity of the
world and the continuity of the nothing.
    Unlike the discourse of the real, which gambles on the
fact of there being something rather than nothing, and
aspires to being founded on the guarantee of an objective
and decipherable world, radical thought, for its part, wagers
on the illusion of the world. It aspires to the status of

illusion, restoring the non-veracity of facts, the non-signification of the world, proposing the opposite hypothesis that there is nothing rather than something, and going in pursuit of that nothing which runs beneath the apparent continuity of meaning. (*PC*, 97–8)

The System of Objects

But to see all this in more detail, we might begin by turning to *The System of Objects* for the third and last time. As we know, *The System of Objects* is ultimately an attempt to classify the possible human relationships to the object, to match objects up with particular social formations and to 'read off' class by the objects consumed. Such projects, of course, had been attempted before – notably by the Frankfurt School (Max Horkheimer, Georg Lukács, Theodor Adorno) and the structuralist sociologists (Kurt Lewin, Talcott Parsons) – but Baudrillard's analysis is more subtle than these. In his study Baudrillard includes not only the actual objects consumed but also aspects of their use, ordering and arrangement. For Baudrillard, the object is not to be comprehended in itself but only in its relationship to its outside. In the functional register of objects, objects are related to other objects, either diachronically in terms of *arrangement* (the successive disposition of objects in time and space) or synchronically in terms of *atmosphere* (the mutually exclusive choice of the colours or materials to make up individual objects). In the non-functional register of objects, objects are related not so much to each other as to a *subject*. They are valued not for their usefulness but for the part they play in an album, set or collection. As Baudrillard says in his Introduction, he will be concerning himself not with objects solely defined by their 'functions or by the categories into which they might be subdivided for analytic purposes, but instead with the processes whereby people relate to them and with the systems of human behaviour and relationships that result therefrom' (*SO*, 4). Despite this, however, he goes on to make the point that this more expanded system of classification still fails, cannot finally reduce the system of objects to a coherent language. Why is this so? Because he would be unable to find a fundamental building block for this system of objects, a 'techneme' (*SO*, 7) that would be the equivalent to a phoneme in language. He writes:

> Whereas a rolled *r* in contrast to a uvular *r* changes nothing so far as the linguistic system is concerned – in other words, the connoted meaning has absolutely no retroactive effect on the denoted structures – the connotation of an object may for its part bring great weight to bear upon technical structures, and alter them significantly. [. . .] The fact that technology depends strictly on the *social* conditions under which technological research is carried out, and hence on the global order of production and consumption, an external contrast which in no way applies to language – all this means that the system of objects, unlike the linguistic system, cannot be described *scientifically* unless it is treated *in the process* as the result of the continual intrusion of a system of practices into a system of techniques. (*SO*, 10)

At first, we might read this as implying a simple richness of consumer behaviour over the available models for it, of practice over theory. It is not any technical specifications that form the basis of the object system – despite such earlier efforts as Gilbert Simondon in his *On the Mode of Existence of Technical Objects* (*SO*, 5–6) – but a 'speech' that always varies, that produces as it were an endless series of dialects and vernaculars. It is just this surplus that Baudrillard attempts to take into account in *The System of Objects* and that would mark his advance over previous efforts. For Baudrillard, there is no real origin to use, no underlying purpose – function, need, symbolic value – that would anchor the system and limit the number of meanings open to the consumer. These things are from the beginning merely tactical or rhetorical devices to be played on to communicate with others. As Baudrillard says: 'The modern home-dweller does not "consume" his objects. [. . .] He dominates, controls and orders them. He discovers himself in the manipulation and tactical equilibration of a system' (*SO*, 26–7). But it is just this which opens up a second and more profound limit to any attempt to construct a system of objects, a limit that unlike the first could never be taken into account. For, as Baudrillard suggests, insofar as these 'consumers' of objects work within a code, the analyst could no sooner propose such a new classification of the system of objects than consumers would play in turn on *this*. That is, if the analyst for his or her part attempts to analyse consumers, these consumers are also analysts. This is why, as Baudrillard says in a statement we first quoted in Chapter 1, not only is every practice of the system of objects an implicit criticism of it, but every criticism is also a form of practice, changes the very thing it seeks to account for: 'The description of the system of objects cannot be divorced from a critique of that system's practical ideology. [. . .] A human science must be a science both of intention and of whatever counters that intention' (*SO*, 10).

In *The System of Objects*, the exact limits this imposes on analysis are left unexplored, but a year after it appeared Baudrillard wrote an essay which took up the difficulties it raised in detail, 'Sign Function and Class Logic', originally published in the semiotics journal *Communications* and now collected in *For a Critique of the Political Economy of the Sign*. It is at this point – even though a year later he was still to write *Consumer Society* with all of its tables and statistics – that we can see Baudrillard first consciously turning against sociology as a discipline. In 'Sign Function and Class Logic', Baudrillard addresses a similar attempt to his own to draw up a classification of objects, that of the American sociologist F. Stuart Chapin in his *Contemporary American Institutions* (*PE*, 33–4). Chapin's project is more modest than Baudrillard's – he ends up reducing his measure merely to the objects found in his respondents' living rooms, and he does not include many aspects of the objects' use – but we can undoubtedly read Baudrillard's comments there as a reflection by him upon the limitations of his own analysis in *The System of Objects*. It is a limit this time not for any contingent reason, the simple excess of practice over theory, which can always be taken into account, but for a necessary reason, a certain excess of theory over practice.

In *Contemporary American Institutions*, Chapin begins his research – typical of many sociological projects at the time – by tabulating a wide variety of objects owned by households and the outside activities undertaken by their families and then trying to match these against their purported social class. Thus, for example, he found that a lack of interior decoration and a low participation in the 'group activities of the community' (1935: 374) corresponded to a 'low' social class, while matched and harmonious furnishing and a high participation in and even financial support of the 'group activities of the community' (1935: 374) corresponded to a 'high' social class. As his research developed, however, Chapin realized that just the list of objects in the living room (and certain aspects of their use) was sufficient to produce the same results. Thus, a kerosene light and softwood floors (1935: 381) in the living room corresponded to people who were skilled or semi-skilled (1935: 393) and earned less than $1,800 a year (1935: 391), while artificial light and hardwood floors (1935: 381) in the living room corresponded to people who were professional or semi-professional (1935: 393) and earned over $1,800 a year (1935: 391).

But Baudrillard in 'Sign Function and Class Logic' makes the point that Chapin's classification fails. First, for an 'objective' reason, which Baudrillard in *The System of Objects* tries to rectify: the fact that, despite Chapin including certain aspects of the use and organization of objects, he still reduces it too much to a matter of mere possession – and it is only in a 'society of relative penury where buying power alone clearly separates the classes' (*PE*, 34) that possession is sufficient to distinguish the different levels of consumers. Thus, the emphasis in *The System of Objects*, in the functional register, on the arrangement and modification of objects and, in the non-functional register, on their belonging to a group or ensemble. But Chapin's classification fails, secondly and more importantly, for a 'subjective' reason, which we can see Baudrillard touching on but not developing in any detail in his Introduction to *The System of Objects*: the fact that, even if we were to add elements of these objects' use and organization, it still remains possible that, once the code is known, far from analysing subjects unconscious of it or the subjects' unconscious, these subjects might consciously manipulate it for their own ends.

That is, the code affects the very thing it is trying to analyse; what the code is attempting to analyse does not exist before it. Here it is not so much too many things and not enough code, as with the first reason, as too much code and not enough things. The code introduces a complexity and possible duplicity to the subjects' behaviour that was not there before it. Baudrillard writes:

> Do not certain objects connote a social membership, a factual status, while others a presumed status, a level of aspirations? Are there 'unrealistic' objects, that is to say, those which falsely register a contradiction of the real status, desperately testifying to an inaccessible standing (all else remaining equal, they are analogous to 'escapist' behaviour or to the utopian behaviours characteristic of critical phases of acculturation)? Conversely, are there witness objects that, despite a mobile status, attest a fidelity to their original class and a tenacious acculturation? Thus there is never a place for listing an inventory of objects and the social significances attached to them: a code in such a case would hardly be more valuable than a 'clef des songes'. It is certain that objects are the carriers of indexed social significations, of a social and cultural hierarchy – and this in the very least of their details: form, material, colours, durability, arrangement in space – in short, it is certain that they constitute a code. But precisely for that reason there is every occasion to think that, far from following the injunctions of this code undeviatingly, individuals and groups use it to their advantage, together with its imperative and distinctive repertory of objects, as is the case with any other institutional and moral code. That is to say, they use it in their own way: they play with it, they break its rules, they speak it with their class dialect. (*PE*, 37)

This second reason, unlike the first, could not be taken into account by a more refined analysis, some renewed attempt to classify the specificities of consumer behaviour. On the contrary, it is just this that opens up the possibility of this behaviour, that subjects, 'far from following the code undeviatingly', might play on it to their own advantage. And, again, even if this self-consciousness on the part of consumers could somehow be factored in by a more subtle analysis, as Baudrillard attempts to do in *The System of Objects*, it is still possible that this analysis would allow yet another play on *it*, and so on. Indeed, in the end it is perhaps not even certain that it is a matter of self-consciousness on the part of these subjects, some deliberate strategy by them to manipulate the code. Although at the time of 'Sign Function and Class Logic', Baudrillard tends to make a distinction between the aristocratic and all other classes in terms of those who manipulate the code and those who are manipulated by it, what is opened up is the possibility that, insofar as this limit is immanent to the code itself, it is not so much subjects who consciously manipulate the code from somewhere outside of it as a certain effect of 'subjectivity' – the objects of the code behaving like subjects – produced by or as the limit to the code. If there is a kind of mental reservation or forethought that produces the seeming match between the code and the subject even where there might be none, there is also a certain ineradicable possibility that even in a proper match between them something is missing, that this is only possible because of a difference between code and reality or this produces a difference between code and reality. That is, it is impossible to distinguish between the two situations Baudrillard raises in that passage above: the first, when the subjects' play on the code is taken into account, and despite their apparent mobility they only 'attest a fidelity to their original class and a tenacious acculturation'; and the second, where the subjects play on this, and their objects 'falsely register a contradiction of the real status'. In other words, pushing Baudrillard's analysis beyond itself, the possibility of a mere conformity to the code is now ineradicable, meaning that just as a play on the code can henceforth be assumed and taken into account, so any seeming obedience to the code can only be read as feigned. That class-based distinction between 'distinction and conformity' (*PE*, 36) becomes impossible to maintain.[1] And it is just this indistinguishability that can be seen undermining the analyses of *The System of Objects* in retrospect, for once the possibility of a deliberate playing on the code is opened up, that first, bourgeois order becomes unlocatable, its inhabitants' apparently unconscious use of objects in terms of their real function only able to be seen as either a holdover inadvertently revealing their true class origins or as a deliberate taking up of outmoded and archaic objects to disguise their proper standing. There is not only no way of actually using objects any more, but no way even of signifying unambiguously through them. There is always something left out by or beyond the code, inaccessible both to the analyst and to the subjects within it.

It is this which is the final paradox of *The System of Objects*, for if it is this 'subjective' practice which ensures there is never a complete short-circuit between the code and what it codifies – Baudrillard's chief complaint against Chapin in 'Sign Function and Class Logic' is that his analysis is a kind of 'vicious circle' (*PE*, 35), in which the analyst simply matches objects up against a class which is already given by them – it is also this 'subjective' practice which means that this classification is never complete, that something always remains to be classified. In a sense, we would want to say that analysis is doubled by this 'subjectivity', but we might put it better by saying that it is this 'subjectivity' itself which stands in for the difference between subject and object that makes their match possible. After the hypothesis of the subject – which is nothing, can always be coded, only has value within the system – the very equivalence between the code and its subject can only be understood for a different reason: either because of a deliberate conformity to the code, 'falsely registering a contradiction of the real status', or because of a 'tenacious acculturation' that goes against the conscious intention of the subject. But again the brilliance of Baudrillard in all of this is that he has found something – the conformity of the subject – that is at once a pure following of the system of objects, something real that can be classified, and a pure fiction that stands in for the difference that makes this classification possible, unreadable by any code. It is something that, after it has been put forward, is unable to be refuted, whose very absence is its proof. The system of classification is ultimately limitless, excludes nothing, but only because of the subject's conformity, the difference between classification and what is classified. Ultimately perhaps, what is revealed is that it is the consumer's – the analyst's – subjectivity as the one thing that can never be classified that is identical to the very system of classification itself; that, as in the collection, each of the objects of classification is a reflection of the analyst's – or consumer's – subjectivity, but this subjectivity itself is always missing.

In the Shadow of the Silent Majorities

We see something of this doubling 'subjectivity' also in Baudrillard's *In the Shadow of the Silent Majorities*. We have already read *In the Shadow* as a continuation of Baudrillard's *Consumer Society*, taking up the question raised there of the circularity between production and waste, solicitation and anguish. We tried to think this in terms of the problem of naming a limit to a system of simulation when this limit is only possible because of the system, only leads to a further extension of it. In the end, we made the point that, if the masses can only lead to an increase in the social, the social itself leads to an increase in the masses. There is only the social, but this only because of the masses. We continue the same line of argument here, but this time we consider the masses in terms not so much of *Consumer Society* as of 'Sign Function and Class Logic', as a limit not so much to the social as to sociology. We look at the masses as a kind of doubling of analysis as such, that difference which makes it at once possible and impossible. And, therefore, we look at the way the masses as this difference are both always represented and unrepresentable, able to be named within the real and what must be excluded to bring it about. *In the Shadow* is certainly a crucial moment in the progressive abstraction of Baudrillard's work, a book where he not only speaks of the limit to simulation, but also, as we saw in Chapter 2, begins to think his own relationship to this limit, how his own writing or theory necessarily takes place within it. It is this limit – the way the masses double Baudrillard's own analysis of them – that we will be addressing here.

We might begin by asking – as we did in Chapter 1 – who or what are the masses? As we responded there, the masses are first of all the underclasses of society, all those for whom society takes it as its task to provide welfare, medicine and education. But perhaps what also needs emphasizing here is that these masses constitute society's image of itself. They are what is common to all members of society, beyond any specifiable group or denomination. They are what none of us sees ourselves as part of, but what each of us in a way belongs to. And they are what we consult and audit in order to know what we as a society think. It is the opinions and attitudes of the masses that all polls and referenda, all surveys and censuses, try to elicit and record: '"The French people think . . .", "The majority of Germans disapprove . . .", "All England thrilled to the birth of the Prince . . ."' (*SSM*, 24). The masses are the one undeniable fact of all sociology and politics, the basic ground on which they stand, the single thing that cannot be doubted. And yet – it is just this paradox or contradiction that *In the Shadow* is organized around – if the masses are the most real, the empirical bedrock of all theories of the social, they are also strangely nebulous, hard to define. There is a sense that, as a sociological category, they are too broad to be of any use, but that in trying to specify them further we lose the very thing we are aiming at. Indeed, it might even be argued that the very attempt to specify the masses is always a mistake, that they can never be made actual but must always remain virtual, both as a sociological concept and as a political force. As Baudrillard writes:

> To want to specify the term 'mass' is a mistake – it is to provide meaning for that which has none. One says: 'the mass of workers'. But the mass is never that of the workers, or of any other social subject or object. [. . .] The mass is without attribute, predicate, quality, reference. This is its definition, or its radical lack of definition. It has no sociological 'reality'. It has nothing to do with any *real* population, body or specific social aggregate. Any attempt to qualify it only seeks to transfer it back to sociology and rescue it from the indistinctness which is not even that of equivalence (the unlimited sum of equivalent individuals: 1 + 1 + 1 – such is the sociological definition), but that of the *neutral*, that is to say *neither one nor the other* (ne-uter). (*SSM*, 5–6)

In other words, what Baudrillard is suggesting here, a little as we saw before in terms of the relationship between the masses and the social, is that the masses are hard to specify or analyse not because they are some concrete reality out there before us – in that case a more subtle analysis would always capture them – but because they are brought about by this analysis itself. There is always something missing from any analysis of the masses, but it is not so much something actual that comes before it as something excluded by this analysis itself. The same gesture that allows us to identify the masses – for, of course, they would not exist even in their nebulousness before their analysis – also makes it impossible. The masses, then – this is the neuter or neutralizing quality Baudrillard speaks of as characterizing them – are at once the most real, the single thing before analysis, and unreal, only a function or fiction of analysis. They are not simply an external limit to our knowledge that would eventually be overcome, but an *internal* limit: the fact that something is always left out to allow us to speak of the masses. It is nothing specific that is excluded – there *are* no masses, as soon as we attempt to speak of them they are lost – but the masses are what is excluded from every theory of the social to allow it to resemble its object. They are excluded to allow the advance of every theory of the social, and even to allow every theory of the social to reflect upon itself and its limits.

So, again, who or what are these masses? In perhaps another way of thinking the masses as neuter, we would say that the masses are not so much anything in themselves as the very relationship *between* things. As we have seen, when sociology speaks of the masses, the masses are not simply out there before it but what allows sociology to speak of the masses, the very relationship between sociology and the masses. And yet, insofar as they are this relationship between themselves and that sociology which studies them, they do not exist before this sociology but only after it, are what sociology could never definitively capture because they come about only as a result of it. That is, the masses are a figure for representation itself.[2] They are not – or not only – something represented but also the difference between things that allows their resemblance, the difference that arises when their resemblance is too close. And Baudrillard makes this connection between the masses and representation in speaking – following 'Sign Function and Class Logic' – of the masses' *conformity*. Let us go back to what we were saying a moment ago about the attempts to describe the masses via opinion polls, surveys, referenda, etc. We said that something was always left out there, not so much because our analysis misses its object as because our analysis *never* misses its object, because the masses do not exist outside of their representation. We get the feeling that in the masses' very fulfilling of our expectations about them there is something we are not quite getting at, that behind their apparent acquiescence something else remains hidden. Baudrillard writes:

> Besides, it is not certain that the procedures of scientific experimentation in the so-called exact sciences have much more truthfulness than surveys and statistics. In any discipline whatsoever, the coded, controlled, 'objective' form of inquiry only allows for this circular type of truth, from which the very object aimed at is excluded. In any case, it is possible to think that the uncertainty surrounding this enterprise of the objective determination of the world remains total and that even matter and the inanimate, when summoned to respond, in the various sciences of nature, in the same terms and according to the same procedures as the masses and 'social' beings in statistics and surveys, also send back the same conforming signals, the same coded responses, with the same exasperating, endless conformity, only the better to escape, in the last instance, exactly like the masses any definition as object. [. . .] But this silence is paradoxical – it isn't a silence which does not speak, it is a silence which *refuses to be spoken in its name*. And in this sense, far from being a form of alienation, it is an absolute weapon. (*SSM*, 32–3, 22)

But this must be read very carefully – and perhaps even against Baudrillard himself. For this is merely to make the masses – like the aristocrats of 'Sign Function and Class Logic' – manipulators of the media from somewhere outside of it. They would be simply what precedes these opinion polls and questionnaires as what they must try to explicate. But, as we have seen, if this is all they were, it is inevitable that the social and sociology would catch up with them, by some series of questions manage to speak their silence. Rather, at the same time the masses are merely a simulation, brought about by this very attempt to survey them and remaining after it. And, similarly, that will seemingly manifested by the match of question to answer is perhaps only an effect of the circular form of the inquiry itself. As in 'Sign Function and Class Logic', there is no need for the hypothesis of a will to account for the masses' conformity: it arises as a structural effect of these surveying techniques themselves. That is, as we saw with the consumers there, even if the masses wanted to give truthful, unevasive answers, they would be unable to because this match between question and answer would always bring about a kind of difference between them, would always leave open the possibility that the masses were merely feigning. What we see, as there, is precisely the indistinguishability between distinction and conformity. The masses do not or do not only exclude themselves from these polls and surveys; they are also only the name for this exclusion. As Baudrillard writes:

> All contemporary systems function on this nebulous entity, on this floating substance whose existence is no longer social, but statistical, and whose only mode of appearance is that of the survey. A simulation on the horizon of the social, or rather on whose horizon the social has already disappeared. [. . .] The mass brings about the same insoluble boundary situation in the field of the 'social'. No longer is it objectifiable (in political terms: no longer is it representable), and it annuls any subject who would claim to comprehend it (in political terms: it annuls anybody who would claim to represent it). Only surveys and statistics (like the law of large numbers and the calculus of possibilities in mathematical physics) can account for it, but one knows that this incantation, this meteoric ritual of statistics and surveys has no real subject, especially not the masses whom it is thought to express. It simply simulates an elusive object, but one whose absence is nevertheless intolerable. It 'produces' it in the form of anticipated responses, of circular signals, which seem to circumscribe its existence and to bear witness to its will. (*SSM*, 19–20, 32–3)

It is the simultaneity of these two positions that is the true paradox of the masses – a simultaneity that, if Baudrillard implies in *In the Shadow*, he does not do quite enough to make clear. The masses are at once before and only after their analysis. Their 'conformity' is both that difference which allows the match between them and that sociology that studies them and is only an effect of this match. They are both that difference that allows us to represent them and only exist after we have represented them.[3] And we see this simultaneity – and the difficulties it raises for analysis – if we look at the masses' ability to imitate or resemble their various descriptions in more detail. On the one hand, this conformity is what all analysts (including Baudrillard) attempt to describe. The masses, when summoned to respond, 'send back the same conforming signals, the same coded responses, with the same, exasperating, endless conformity' as objects in the physical sciences. What is essential to the masses is their conformity, the way they endlessly re-affirm our image of them, like a 'mirror held out for an ever blind, ever absent recognition' (*SSM*, 24), 'sending back to the system its own logic by doubling it, reflecting meaning without absorbing it' (*SSM*, 108). But, on the other hand, if the masses conform to the various theories about them, they also would not be masses, there would be nothing for these theories to describe, until *after* there was something for them to conform to, until *after* there had been some attempt to account for them. That is, if theory imitates or describes something – those masses which conform – it also imitates or describes nothing; these masses that conform would not exist until after that theory which attempts to conform to them. It is impossible to say which comes first: the masses which conform to their theories or these theories which conform to the masses. In order to explain how the masses conform to their theory, we already need a theory that has tried to conform to the masses. In order to explain how theory conforms to the masses, we already need a masses that have tried to conform to their theory. In any attempt to explain how conformity takes place, we already need a conformity before this and, thus, if conformity always takes place too soon, it also takes place too late. If we attempt to conform to the masses because the masses already conform to us, the masses only conform to us because we already conform to them.[4]

All of this is to suggest that what *In the Shadow* – like all of Baudrillard's work – is about is representation. What Baudrillard is trying to describe by the masses is not so much anything as such as description itself. He is trying to represent representation. For, once more, who or what are the masses? They are neither simply real nor our description of them but the very relationship between the two, what allows them to resemble each other. The masses are not so much real as the conformity that allows us to resemble the real. The real masses are not so much the masses we describe as what is between us and the masses we describe. This is why again the masses both precede any attempt to describe them as that representation or conformity that allows this and come about only after our attempts to describe them as that representation or conformity thereby created. As with seduction, the paradox of the masses is that we must try not simply to describe the masses but to occupy the very relationship between the masses and their description, as the masses do themselves. And the question in *In the Shadow* is to what extent Baudrillard realizes this, that it is possible the masses only conform to his own description of them, arise as an effect of it, that he speaks only of himself when he speaks of the masses. Baudrillard wants to say that 'no one speaks for the masses' silence' (*SSM*, 22), that the 'masses should not be transferred into meaning' (*SSM*, 40–1), and yet this is just what he does, even in saying this. This conformity of the masses would not exist until after Baudrillard attributes this quality to them; but it is just this conformity that reduces any attempt to discuss them to paradox or contradiction, that means the criticism Baudrillard makes of others in speaking of the masses also applies to him. The masses double *all* discourse about them, even Baudrillard's own, explain it for a completely different reason, so that it represents what it does only because of the difference between it and what it represents, represents what it does only because it does not represent it.

In the Shadow carries on and develops that argument concerning the sign we saw all the way ago in *The System of Objects*. It is a sign that, if it allows us to say what something is insofar as we are able to exchange it for something else, also means that we cannot say what anything is because we can only exchange it for something else. *In the Shadow* attempts to think through what is excluded by this logic of the sign. It seeks to grasp the thing itself, the object before the sign, but of course it could only say what it is through the sign. It is this thing that is excluded so that signs can exchange themselves for each other through it. And this thing is precisely the *real*. What *In the Shadow* is ultimately about – at once singular and universal, the one thing before the sign and only an effect of it, what every sign stands in for and what is excluded by each of them – is the real. And – this has been our argument throughout – what Baudrillard is doing here is defending the real against all attempts to represent it (including his own). It is a real that is the limit to all systems, a real that no system could ever entirely capture or explain. And yet, again, this real is only the paradox that the closer representation comes to the thing it resembles the less it resembles it. It is this point at which absolute resemblance and absolute difference touch that Baudrillard means by the real. It is on the basis of this real that Baudrillard constructs his own theory and it is by means of it that he is able to double any theory, show that the resemblance it constructs between it and its object is only possible for another reason it does not see: the very difference between them. But this real upon which the system cannot reflect, which it can never capture or explain, is only the sign itself. What stranger hypothesis, what more uncanny doubling, could there be than this? As Baudrillard writes: 'In the last analysis, object and subject are one. We can only grasp the essence of the world if we can grasp, in all its irony, the truth of this radical equivalence' (*PC*, ii).

* * *

That the world conforms, that behind its seeming appearance another intention is hidden or that behind its apparent progress another destiny is taking place: this is Baudrillard's essential argument. And for him it is the way thought itself works.

Theory, criticism, writing, is not a matter of adducing evidence, weighing up the alternatives before deciding on one of them. Why? Because there is no other to the systems he analyses, no evidence he can give that does not go towards them. There is no outside standard by which to judge them, no 'ought' he can oppose to 'is' (*PC*, 65). Rather, it is a matter of bringing these two opposites immediately together. We do not say that the system we are looking at is partly true but partly false, raise some empirical limit to it that the system would always overcome, but say that the system has no limits only because it excludes its object. As Baudrillard puts it in *Cool Memories I*:

> It is a stroke of wit. The stroke of wit also despairs of language, but from that despair it always derives a brilliant simplification, drawing a line between two diametrically opposed poles. A diabolical solution; everything is in the ellipsis. There is no crueller trick you can play on reality than to idealize it just as it is. (*CM I*, 175)

And, therefore, it is not a matter of persuasion or argument, of convincing the other of this, because this 'solution' is unthinkable, nonsensical, imageless. Once said, however, it is undeniable. The very fact that the system is limitless – that there is no other to it – becomes its proof. We do not argue empirically against the system – for there is no evidence against it, the system is fundamentally not empirical – but rather to the doubling of the system we oppose our own doubling. We do not – or not only – offer a description of the way things are, but a *prescription* of the way they will be. It is a matter not of a gradual enunciation in the real but of a sudden *annunciation* in the virtual, after which everything is at once the same and completely different. Again *Cool Memories I*:

> Theory does not derive its legitimacy from established facts, but from future events. Its value is not in the past events it can illuminate, but in the shockwave of the events it prefigures. It does not act upon consciousness, but directly on the course of things from which it draws its energy. (*CM I*, 215)

This is the power, the singular power, of thought. It is not to fight against the world, not to speak against it, but to explain it in an entirely other way. It is not logical, linear – these are the very qualities of simulation it opposes – but works via reversibility, ellipsis, anamorphosis. It does not attempt to see this world from another world, another perspective, but seeks to discover another world, another perspective, already in this one (*PC*, 96). It is an attempt to speak, as we have seen Baudrillard try to in *The Perfect Crime*, of that 'nothing' excluded to make this world possible; but it is a nothing that is itself only visible because of this world. It is to show each time that something is missing from the system examined, but missing only after it has been repeated by theory. Theory is only a kind of supplement to the real, but reality would not be without this supplement; reality becomes the supplement to theory: 'Illusion [theory] is made up of this magic portion, this accursed share which creates a kind of absolute surplus-value by the subtraction of causes or by the distortion of effects and causes' (*PC*, 58). This again is Baudrillard's strategy: by simply following the system to the end, adding nothing to it, he at the same time doubles it, shows that it comes about for an entirely different reason. Or, at least, he makes it undecidable which comes first: the reality of the system or the always virtual, undemonstrable yet irrefutable, 'illusion' of theory.

How to think this unthinkable, these 'empty, illegible, insoluble' (*EC*, 59) signs, which do not have a 'subject of enunciation, or an enounced' (*EC*, 60), and which go beyond the one who thinks them? This is the paradoxical aspect of thought: that it aims at something beyond itself, which cannot be thought, some moment when language outruns thought or thought resembles nothing. But it is at just this moment too that thought most resembles this world which similarly is beyond itself, resembles nothing. This is why – in a sense beyond Baudrillard – it is a matter not simply of breaking with resemblance, of a pure sacrifice of thought, but, rather, as we saw with seduction, of the *economy* of this loss. Thought aims at something beyond it, wants to lose itself, but it is precisely when it is most free, most like itself or even beyond itself, that it is most like the world, follows the world most closely. Thought is most free when it is bound to the world and most bound to the world when it is most free. And the dilemma for criticism therefore is that it cannot tell whether it is truly critical of the world or only the repetition of a world that is already critical of itself. This is the question of the meaning and destiny of criticism that Baudrillard raises in his last books. As he writes in *The Ecstasy of Communication*: 'What is the point of saying that the world *is* ecstatic, that it *is* ironic, that the world *is* objective? It is these things, that's that' (*EC*, 100). Or in *The Perfect Crime*: 'We cannot project more order or disorder into the world than there is. We cannot transform it more than it transforms itself' (*PC*, 10). Again, against the idea of actually changing the world or judging it from the outside, there is the admission of a kind of immanence. And yet, as Baudrillard also says:

> What lends writing, fictional or theoretical, its intensity is the void, the nothingness running beneath the surface, the illusion of meaning, the ironic dimension of language, correlative with that of the facts themselves, which are never anything but what they are. That is to say, they are never more than what they are and they are, literally, never only what they are. The irony of the facts, in their wretched reality, is precisely that they are only what they are but that, by that very fact, they are necessarily beyond. (*PC*, 98)

What does Baudrillard mean by this? That things are as they are only because they are represented, only come into being across the void or nothingness of representation. At the same time as this representation enables them to be what they are – so what is the point of saying that? – they are henceforth only for an absolutely different reason, because they stand in for that nothing or void it introduces into the world. In merely repeating what is, language inverts it, makes it seem as though things come about only because of it. In retracing the world, it subtracts something, makes it seem as though the world has always been waiting for its writing to complete itself (*CM I*, 35).

But each time, as we say, this limit that thought introduces into the world – this limit that thought thinks, that is perhaps thought itself – is the limit of representation. It is that the world must be represented. This is why, as Baudrillard says, illusion is more powerful than reality, for reality is ultimately only possible because it is represented. And each time Baudrillard has to rediscover for the system he investigates the figure for this representation. Each time he must both create and stand in for, repeat and in repeating bring about for the first time, that difference which allows representation. This is the challenge for Baudrillard, to find at once a reproducible rule that plays out an order already in the world and something unexpected that is beyond any order or rule. It is the difficulty of this book too, for there can finally be no sequence to it or logic to the separation of its chapters. Baudrillard repeats the same essential paradox throughout his work, his argument is already fully expressed in *The System of Objects* and it is still being made in *The Perfect Crime*; but at the same time each text is different, there is no way of predicting in advance what form it will take, the very object in which this problematic is found is not different from its 'solution'. In a way, that is, it is never entirely there, we can never exactly say what Baudrillard is doing, his underlying argument is never to be found separate from its examples. Each time, however, the system he looks at corresponds to its limits, the system *is* its limit. At once the system is only possible because of its end, brings it about, and is the very deferral or impossibility of its end, this end is only possible because of the system. The system and its end are simultaneous or occur at the same time. This is precisely that *trait d'esprit*, exchange, doubling, at the heart of the world and thought. It is at once beyond thought and what makes thought possible, what must remain unthought and what thought stands in for.

The Evil Demon of Images

To conclude this chapter, we might look at how this doubling is worked out in two specific cases. The first is a little known text of Baudrillard's, not quite part of his official oeuvre, *The Evil Demon of Images* of 1984. *Evil Demon*, like 'The Orders of Simulacra' and 'The Precession of Simulacra', is another attempted history of simulation, this time told in terms of so-called 'iconic' images, images that bear some analogical relationship to what they represent (photography, film, television). Like those other histories Baudrillard narrates, it is the story of the gradual loss of the difference between the copy and the referent, and hence the growing independence between them. It is this difference that both allows their resemblance and arises when they resemble each other too closely that Baudrillard calls the 'evil demon' of images after the famous *'malin génie'* of René Descartes's *Meditations*. And it is the loss of this difference between the copy and the original that is particularly a problem for these iconic images because by their very nature they are already so close to the thing they represent. As Baudrillard writes, characterizing this evil demon in terms of its power of conformity or illusion:

> It is precisely when it appears most truthful, most faithful and most in conformity to reality that the image is most diabolical – and our technical images, whether they be from photography, cinema or television, are in the overwhelming majority much more 'figurative', 'realist', than all the images from past cultures. It is in its resemblance, not only analogical but technological, that the image is most immoral and most perverse. (*ED*, 13–14)

More specifically, *Evil Demon* traces the passage of these media images from the first order of simulacra, where image and reality are linked by a kind of difference, to the second order of simulacra, where they have nothing in common, to the third order of simulacra, where the image speaks of the difference between it and reality and reality only arises as an effect of the image. With regard to the first order, Baudrillard looks at early examples of mass media images (primitive film, photography, even museum dioramas). We see in them, as in Baroque stucco and *trompe l'oeil*, a crudity and poverty of means, a distance from the real, that allows the play of the spectator's imagination, a place for him or her within the work. They do not seek directly to represent the real, but merely to evoke it (*ED*, 33). Baudrillard contrasts here the static theatricality of the slides at the New York Museum of Natural History depicting the Ice Age to

the cinematic verisimilitude of the film *The Day After*, which
attempts to show the consequences of a future nuclear war:

> The slides at the New York Museum of Natural History move
> me much more profoundly [than *The Day After*]: you can
> shiver at the Ice Age and feel the charm of the prehistoric,
> but here I feel neither the shiver nor the charm of nuclear
> power, nor even suspense or the final blinding flash. (*ED*,
> 26–7)

With regard to the second order, Baudrillard looks at a series of
recent Hollywood films which at once attempt to capture
the minutiae of everyday life and experience – 'the real, the
immediate, the unsignified' (*ED*, 33) – in a way never seen
before and to re-create perfectly previous genres of cinema. But
it is just at this point that these films no longer have anything to
do with reality or even these originals. They lose their power to
move us or to involve us in them, not because they are no good
but because they are *too* good (*ED*, 32). As Baudrillard says of
the film *The Last Picture Show*, which is a flawless imitation of
a 1950s teenage rebel genre film:

> You need only to be sufficiently distracted, as I was, to see it
> as a 1950s original production: a good film of manners and
> the ambience of small town America, etc. A slight suspicion:
> it was a little too good, better adjusted, better than the
> others, without the sentimental, moral and psychological tics
> of the films of that period. (*ED*, 31)

Finally, with regard to the third order, Baudrillard looks at a
number of films that appear once again to open themselves up
to the real only to make the real over in their image, close the
real off more than ever. Baudrillard cites as an example of this
the television series *Holocaust*, which in purporting to tell the
'forgotten' story of the concentration camps in Nazi Germany,
something that is truly real, beyond representation, only continues – and possibly initiates – the same forgetting: 'But in
effect what is thus exorcized so cheaply, at the cost of a few
tears [our collective guilt at Auschwitz], will never recur
because it is presently happening in the very form through
which it is denounced, through the very medium of this supposed exorcism: television' (*ED*, 24). Or Baudrillard cites as

another example of this production of the real the film *The China Syndrome*, where a fictional dramatization of a meltdown at a nuclear plant was followed a few weeks later by a real-life accident at Harrisburg, so that now even the nuclear can only be imagined in the mode of the televisual: 'The film is a fine example of the supremacy of the televised event over the nuclear event, which itself remains improbable and in some sense imaginary' (*ED*, 19).

Thus, as in 'The Orders of Simulacra' and 'The Precession of Simulacra', Baudrillard is setting forth in *Evil Demon* all the consequences of simulation, including the consequence that there is no simple way of speaking of what is outside of it because this outside is only possible because of simulation. But perhaps in *Evil Demon* there is a more complicated thinking through of the consequences of this for Baudrillard's own critical position (though, once again, this is not addressed directly but only allegorically). As we have said, Baudrillard compares this difference or illusion necessary for resemblance to Descartes's evil demon, and like Descartes he uses this to reflect upon what he can and cannot know. That is, in a gesture that in a way repeats Descartes, Baudrillard begins to consider that even his ability to think the illusion of the evil demon might be itself only another illusion of this demon. But, of course, to the extent that he cannot name what is outside or before simulation, there is a certain limit to thinking *this*; he cannot even be certain that this illusion has occurred. Indeed, we might even go on to say that the very proof of simulation is that we cannot think it, cannot say it has taken place. This is what Baudrillard says about the film *Holocaust*: that 'forgetting the extermination (by means of its simulation in the televised version) is part of the extermination itself' (*ED*, 23). And it is also what he says of the film *The Day After*, in which the real end of the world is not its supposed nuclear annihilation but the fact that we are no longer able to imagine this end, that this end is now only imaginable in simulated form: 'It is *it* [*The Day After*] which *is* our catastrophe. It does not represent it; it does not evoke it. On the contrary, it shows that it has already happened, that it is already here, since it is impossible to imagine' (*ED*, 27; see also *CM I*, 136). It is in this sense again that simulation is not a real phenomenon, does not take place in the real, but is rather a *doubling* of the world. Henceforth, after the hypothesis of simulation, things just as they are – real Indians in the forest, unspoilt and unpolluted nature – can only be explained because of it. The fact that there is no end to the world, that we cannot think its end, is precisely proof of the end of the world by simulation.

This absolute doubt that simulation plunges the analyst into is like that of the evil demon for Descartes, where any reflection upon the problem might only be a reflection of the problem, where any naming of the evil demon might only be a product of the evil demon itself. But, as is well known, it is just from this realization that Descartes, in a manoeuvre crucial for philosophy, derives a sort of certainty, a position from which to stand outside of this illusion. For, he says, even if all is illusion and even if thinking about this may be an illusion, he can at least *know* this and by this means obtain a kind of certainty. That is, it is in thinking about his limits that he in a sense overcomes them. He implicitly contains a sense of perfection, a kind of God within, insofar as he can reflect upon his own failings and imperfections. He might never have this perfect intelligence himself, but insofar as he is able to think his own doubt another or another's certainty is implied. As Descartes writes in his *Meditations*:

> Nothing else in me is so perfect or so great but that I cannot understand the possibility of something still more perfect, still greater. If I consider the faculty of understanding, I discover at once that in me it is very slight and greatly restricted. I thereupon form the idea of a far greater faculty, indeed, of the greatest possible, an infinite one; and I perceive from the mere fact that I can form an idea of this that it belongs to the nature of God. (1977: 95)[5]

But Baudrillard in *Evil Demon* argues that he goes beyond Descartes – or that the Cartesian gesture of certainty is no longer open – in that he is not wanting finally to deduce a principle of certainty, but to think through to the very end the limits to thought posed by simulation, up to the fact that part of its effect is that we precisely cannot think it, that every thinking of it (even thinking that we cannot think it) is open to doubt. Doubt, illusion, the evil demon – we might say the difference between things – is anterior to certainty, reality, resemblance. Every certainty – even the certainty of doubt – is open to a further doubt. This is what Baudrillard says in an interview at the end of *Evil Demon*, contrasting his project with that of Descartes:

> For me the question is totally different. When I invoke the principle of evil, of an evil demon, etc., my aim is more closely related to a certain kind of Manichaeism (than it is to Descartes). It is therefore anterior to Descartes, and fundamentally it is *ir*rational. There are in fact two principles at stake: on the one hand, there is the (Descartes') rational principle or principle of rationality – the fundamental attempt, through doubt or anything else, to rationalize the world – and, on the other hand, there is the inverse principle, which was, for example, adopted by 'heretics' all the way throughout the history of Christianity. This is the principle of evil itself. What the heretics posited was that the very creation of the world, hence the reality of the world, was the result of the existence of the evil demon. The function of God, then, was really to try to repudiate this evil phantom – that was the real reason why God had to exist at all. So in this situation it is no longer a question of doubt or non-doubt, of whether one should exercise this doubt or whether this doubt could lead us to confirm or deny the existence of the world. Rather, it is once again the principle of *seduction* that needs to be invoked in this situation: according to Manichaeism, the reality of the world is a total illusion; it is something which has been tainted from the very beginning; it is something which has been seduced by a sort of *ir*real principle since time immemorial. (*ED*, 43–4)

Yet in a way that Baudrillard does not see, he cannot help repeating Descartes's fundamental strategy of turning doubt into certainty. For if Baudrillard says he cannot think simulation, that simulation comes before any thinking of it, he can at least think *this*. If he says he cannot name the evil demon as the difference between things that allows their resemblance because any such naming would be subject to this difference (*BL*, 112), he can at least name this failure as that of the *evil demon*. If he says simulation can no longer be seen as such but is proven in its absence, he can at least name this absence as *simulation*. To put it another way, if this all-inclusiveness and lack of an other is evidence of simulation, the very fact that it can be named as such is also its limit. For insofar as it can be named – to paraphrase Descartes's argument for the existence of God – there is implied a power greater than it, that difference between us and it which allows it to be represented. In other words, to the extent we are able to name our limits as simulation, we are able to pass outside of them: it is no longer our self-consciousness or subjectivity (as Descartes at first can be seen to be saying), or even God (as Descartes in a closer reading is saying), but representation, that difference that allows all things to be represented – doubt, the self, God – that offers us a final basis of certainty. It is this doubling power of representation in its ability to represent the world as simulacrum that necessarily implies a power greater than it. It is a power of representation which, if it is subjective, belongs to the will of the thinker, also goes beyond him or her, of which he or she would be merely the effect. This again for Baudrillard is the power of language, representation itself, which, if it is the problem – creates the world as a simulacrum, allows us to think the world as a simulacrum – is also the solution, allows us to think, or at least represent, some power outside of it which makes it possible. And this process of doubling can go on for ever. Insofar as simulation is able to be thought, it can be doubled by Baudrillard's evil demon. Insofar as Baudrillard's evil demon is able to be represented, it too is able to be doubled. Thought ultimately – as Baudrillard says in *The Perfect Crime* – takes place in the name of a certain nothing, a nothing that makes the world and everything within it possible. But, as he also says there, this 'crime' is never perfect, always leaves traces, this nothing is always something – and insofar as it is, insofar as we can think it at all, it is always able to be doubled by another. We are at once always breaking with Descartes and always repeating him.

'The Year 2000 Will Not Take Place'

To conclude, we give another example both of this doubling by simulation and of how simulation is always able to be doubled. We look here at the essay 'The Year 2000 Will Not Take Place' (also intriguingly titled 'The Year 2000 Has Already Happened' (Baudrillard, 1987)), a version of which is reprinted in *The Illusion of the End*. *The Illusion of the End* is a series of interlinked essays that is discussed, if only briefly, by a number of Baudrillard's commentators in terms of the 'end of things'. Thus the American Social Historian Martin Jay speaks of 'Baudrillard's preoccupation with the end of history and the general melancholy which pervades things today as evidence of a profound nihilistic despair which runs through "post-modern" thinking at the fin-de-millennium' (Bogard, 1994: 315). And the American German and Film Studies scholar Laurence Rickels writes: 'The unstoppable mania of this text's virulent attack on the body of opinion [. . .] is a literally conservative project or projection' (1993: 12). But we would say that 'The Year 2000' is beyond any simple argument for the end of things, even against such thinkers as Derrida in his 'Of an Apocalyptic Tone Recently Adopted in Philosophy', which obviously alludes to Baudrillard amongst others. Indeed, we would say that what we see in Baudrillard's work is a thinking of 'closure' as opposed to 'end', to use Derrida's own distinction.[6] 'The Year 2000' is not so much an essay on the end of things – history, the social, music – as on their simultaneously enabling and disenabling conditions. It is a meditation upon the relationship of history to the events it wants to speak of – events perhaps by definition marking the beginning or end of something, a moment in the present. What is the relationship of history to this event, this now? How is this event what makes history possible and yet what is impossible within it? How does history stand in for this event and how does this event double history? And, finally, what is the relationship between Baudrillard's speculations concerning the end of history in the first half of his essay and the two different kinds of time he discusses in the second half? These are the abstract issues Baudrillard raises in 'The Year

2000', and which go well beyond any direct millennialism or call for the end of things.

Baudrillard begins 'The Year 2000' with a quotation from Elias Canetti's *The Human Province*:

> A painful thought: that beyond a certain precise moment in time, history is no longer real. Without realizing it, the whole human race suddenly left reality behind. Nothing that has occurred since then has been true, but we are unable to realize it. Our task and our duty now is to discover this point or, so long as we fail to grasp it, we are condemned to continue on our present destructive course. ('2000', 18)

Baudrillard will agree with Canetti's diagnosis, but disagree with his prescription of somehow trying to find a way back to that point at which reality was lost. Baudrillard in 'The Year 2000' offers three 'hypotheses' ('2000', 18) – between which importantly he does not choose – to try to explain why history has ended. The first is that today things happen too quickly, are over before they begin: 'Events no longer have consequences because they go too quickly – they are diffused too quickly, too far, they are caught up in circuits – they can never return as testimony for themselves or their meaning (meaning is always a testimony)' ('2000', 19). The second is the inverse of the first. It is not that events occur too quickly but too slowly, not that the end seems to take place before the beginning or is already there in the beginning, but that the event never actually reaches its end, cannot get from its beginning to its end. Baudrillard writes:

> Progress, history, reason, desire are no longer able to find their 'escape velocity'. They can no longer pull away from this too dense body which irresistibly slows their progress [. . .]. History can no longer outrun itself, it can no longer envisage its own finality, dream of its own end; it is buried in its immediate effect, it implodes in the here and now. Finally, we cannot even speak of the end of history because *there is no time* for it to reach its own end. ('2000', 20–1)

Baudrillard's third hypothesis is slightly different from the first two. Baudrillard takes his analogy this time not from the imagary of astrophysics but from music. In a sense, it is a repetition of that paradox of representation we have spoken of throughout this book: history ends because it is now too close to the events it wants to recount, not because it has lost touch with them but because it is indistinguishable from them. Baudrillard compares this to the current perfection in the reproduction of music in stereo (and Baudrillard is writing in 1984, even before the current revolution in compact disc technology). We might say that it is exactly in coming too close to its original music that stereo loses something of it, that henceforth stereo no longer resembles music but only itself or music is only able to be imagined in terms of the model stereo provides. Baudrillard writes:

> We are all obsessed (and not only in music) with high fidelity, obsessed with the quality of musical 'reproduction'. Armed with the tuners, amplifiers and speakers of our stereo systems, we adjust bass and treble, we mix, we combine, we multiply tracks, in search of an impeccable technology and an infallible music. I still remember a sound booth in a recording studio where the music, broadcast on four tracks, reached you in four dimensions, so that it seemed visceral, secreted from the inside, with a surreal depth . . . This was no longer music. Where is the degree of technological sophistication, where is the 'high fidelity' threshold beyond which music as such would disappear? For the problem of the disappearance of music is the same as that of the disappearance of history: it will not disappear *for want of* music, it will disappear for having exceeded that limit point, vanishing point, it will disappear in the perfection of its materiality, in its own special effect (beyond which there is no longer any aesthetic judgement or aesthetic pleasure, it is the ecstasy of musicality and its end). ('2000', 21; see also *CM I*, 82–3; *CM II* on CDs, 56–7)

This is what happens to the 'little music' of history too: 'it disappears in the excessive reference (which functions as "deterrence", dissuasion), it vanishes in the microscopy, in the instantaneousness of information, it too is seized by the uncertainty principle' ('2000', 22). But it is at this point that we might pause for a moment and ask a question that has often been posed by Baudrillard's commentators: how is it that Baudrillard can say that it is 'music' that is lost by stereo? Does not stereo better than ever reproduce music? Can we not only hear music through stereo? Is Baudrillard not being nostalgic here, or contradicting his own argument, when he speaks of music being lost by stereo? In short, what is it that Baudrillard means by this 'music as such' that disappears? In one way, Baudrillard *does* actually mean that music is excluded by the system of stereo. By this he might mean the spontaneous, improvisational quality of music, the sense of hearing it for the first time. He might mean that in a too pure recording process we lose the distortion, crackle and hiss that add so much atmosphere to music. And yet, in another way, Baudrillard cannot mean actual music, some real quality that is excluded from stereo, or it is certainly nothing we could hear. Even if it is the crackle and hiss, some indefinable 'atmosphere', that is missing from music, this can and is being put back in today. But this 'supplementary simulation' ('2000', 22) is only to exclude music all the more, is only to drive music further away than ever. Baudrillard, that is, does not oppose stereo but *doubles* it, gives it an entirely different explanation than its own. Stereo is at least potentially perfect, but this only because it has excluded its music, this only to exclude its music. And this 'music' is a kind of nothing, a pure limit that can be stated if not thought or heard (but indeed it can be thought and heard after it is stated). Stereo is only possible because of the distance between it and its music, and once this line is crossed it no longer reproduces music at all. The same limit that means that stereo is total also means that it is not.

We see this if we return to Baudrillard's third hypothesis concerning the end of history. History has ended for Baudrillard, despite the way this is understood by his commentators, not because there is too little history, because something is actually lost from history, but because there is *too much* history, because there is no longer any distance between history and the events it records. That is, as with music, history does not simply come to an end; we cannot say what is lost from history. And it is for this reason that Baudrillard differs from Canetti, who, if he speaks about reality suddenly being lost, can also urge us to go back to the way things were, as though one of the effects of this loss of reality were not our inability to think it. Or, indeed, as though any attempt to do so, to go back to reality or history as it was before, were not itself only possible because of simulation, only to lead to an increase in simulation. As though the attempt to find a real history, a real music, were not the very problem itself. Here, against those who accuse him of nostalgia, Baudrillard is thinking through the effects of the loss of the real, how to speak against simulation, when there is no real but only simulation:

> The crossing of this unidentifiable point (the end of history) is therefore irreversible (contrary to what Canetti implicitly hopes). The situation suddenly becomes entirely novel. We can no longer discover music as it was before stereo (unless by an effect of supplementary simulation), we can no longer discover history as it was before information and the media. The original essence (of music, of the social . . .), the original concept (of the unconscious, of history . . .) have disappeared because we can never again isolate them from their model of perfection, which at the same time is their model of simulation, of their forced assumption in an excessive truth, which at once is their point of inertia and their point of no-return. We will never know what was the social, or what was music before their present exacerbation in useless perfection. We will never know what history was before its exacerbation in the technical perfection of information or its disappearance in the profusion of commentary – we will never know what anything was before its disappearance in the completion of the model . . . Such is the era of simulation. ('2000', 22–3)

However, if simulation is irrefutable, if any outside to it is only conceivable because of it, at the same time the statement that makes this possible also makes it impossible. The very statement which means there is no outside to simulation, that simulation is total, also means there is an outside to simulation, that simulation is not total. For let us look – as in *Evil Demon* – at Baudrillard's arguments regarding the all-inclusiveness of simulation. Against Canetti, he says we cannot think the loss of the real. In characterizing simulation, he says we cannot know what music and history were before their 'forced assumption in an excessive truth, which at once is their point of inertia and their point of no-return'. But, of course, if Baudrillard breaks with Canetti, as he breaks with Descartes in *Evil Demon*, in saying that we can no longer think the loss of the real, we can at least think *this*. If on the one hand we cannot say what music and history were before simulation, on the other we can at least think they were different, that something is lost, we can at least say we have not got these things now. But the crucial thing to realize here is that the same statement that means simulation is total, that there is no other to it, that it doubles, also means it is not, that it must be explained for another reason, that it can be doubled. To the very extent that we are able to say it is *stereo* and the *end of history* that are proved in their absence, this is only to stand in for the real thing that is proved in its absence and that allows these to stand in for it: the very difference between things, representation itself. And all of this is ultimately only to stand in for the very 'nothingness' of the world, which at once has already occurred and never actually takes place, is there to allow all representation and is excluded by any representation, is a pure nothingness and only the space between things, is perfect and imperfect.[7]

It is at this point that we might turn to the second half of 'The Year 2000', in which Baudrillard puts forward – in a seemingly unrelated gesture – a certain argument about the emergence of linear time or history itself (again, the whole question of how he could say this, how he could speak of the emergence as well as the end of history when history is over). Baudrillard begins there by distinguishing between two different types of time: the first, the 'ceremonial' time of 'primitive' societies, 'where everything is completed in the beginning and where the ceremony retraces the perfection of this original event – perfect in the sense that everything is complete' ('2000', 23); the second, the linear time of Christian and modern societies, in which 'events are thought to follow one another like cause and effect', and in which even the 'eschatological process, Last Judgement or revolution, salvation or catastrophe, is at once the time of the end and of its unlimited suspension' ('2000', 23). Baudrillard does not simply choose between these two times, but rather plots the emergence of the second out of the first and the continuing struggle between them, between that linear history in which the end is always deferred, the promised Kingdom always in the next world, and the defiance of history, the attempt to bring the end closer, to make the beginning and end the same. As Baudrillard says, speaking of these two contradictory forces that emerge with the notion of linear time or that perhaps together make up time itself:

> Two contradictory forces arise with linear time, i.e., with the birth of time as such. The first consists in following the meanderings of this time and in constructing a history, the other consists in accelerating the course of time, or in abruptly condensing it to bring it to an end. Opposed to the historical perspective, which constantly displaces the stakes onto a hypothetical end, has always been a fatal demand, a fatal strategy of time, which is to leap ahead, to annihilate time and to short-circuit the Last Judgement. It cannot be said that either of these two forces has truly triumphed over the other, and throughout history the burning question remains: should we or should we not wait? ('2000', 24)

It is at this point that we might go back to Baudrillard's three 'hypotheses' – between which again, importantly, he does not choose – concerning the end of history and try to make a connection. For what is it that Baudrillard is really speaking about here in this struggle between cyclical and linear time, that time which brings the end closer and that time which defers it? And why in a sense does he not want to choose between these two forms of time? Why, if linear time appears to have triumphed, can he not say this definitively? Why throughout history are there outbreaks – momentary, apocryphal, without lasting effects – of other kinds of time? Let us think for a moment about the structure of time, and more particularly about Zeno's famous paradoxes of motion which are also paradoxes of time. What is it that Zeno is saying there? He says that we cannot get from point A to point B because there is always between them another point C, and between A and C another point D, and so on. In this way, he is able to show that motion, time understood as a series of points strung together, is impossible. He is able to argue that we cannot get from beginning to end, that the end is forever deferred, because there is always another point between us and the end. But if Zeno is thereby able to disprove motion, it is only by having to assume it, for in order to demonstrate why we cannot get to the end he has to suppose we are already there: *before we get to the end*, there would always be a point halfway between us and the end. In other words, Zeno does not so much disprove motion as reveal it is self-contradictory, does not so much disprove motion as its merely linear conception. That is, what Zeno finally shows is that in order for motion to be possible we cannot simply understand its beginning and end as separate, because then we could not explain how we get from one to the other. The two must be connected, the end already in the beginning. But if this is what makes motion possible, it also makes it impossible, for, as we have seen, it is precisely on this basis (that we at the beginning can get to the end or are already at the end) that the endless division of space between the beginning and end is possible, that we are unable to get from one to the other.

We can state this paradox more directly in terms of time, for here too there is a similar problem. We can speak of one moment simply following another, of one moment coming to take the place of or substituting for the other, but in this case is it this next moment that appears to allow the previous one to disappear or that previous moment that disappears to allow the next to appear? In order to have this linear passage of one moment to another, we must imagine, impossibly, a time in which both are present, in which two times are at the same time, in which the first disappears as the second appears. Again that second moment is already in the first; but it is also this which enables the constant interposition of another moment between this first and second, the ceaseless unwinding of time without end. That is, there are always as it were two times, the one virtual, which we never experience, in which all moments are co-present, the other actual, which is the only way we can grasp or experience time, in which one moment comes after the other. We can only grasp time linearly, but this only because of a certain circularity. This circularity is at once what makes

linear time possible and impossible (because in it there is no
progress from one moment to the next, because it is on its
basis that there is the endless deferral of that last moment).
And it is in this sense that we must understand Baudrillard's
insistence that, although linear time has appeared to triumph, it
cannot finally be separated from cyclical time. Both that
endless deferral of the end we have in linear time is only
possible because the end is already in the beginning as in
ceremonial time and that equivalence of beginning and end we
have in ceremonial time, can only be experienced as the
succession of one moment after another of linear time. And
time itself is both of these. The paradox of time, what is
required for it, is neither simply the linear deferral of the end –
too slow – nor the cyclical end already in the beginning – too
fast – but both. As Baudrillard writes:

> A certain slowness (that is to say a certain speed, but not
> too much), a certain distance but not too much, a certain
> 'liberation' (or energy of rupture and change) but not too
> much, in order that this kind of significative condensation or
> crystallization of events that we call history be produced,
> this kind of coherent succession of causes and effects that
> we call the real. ('2000', 18)

But, importantly, it is not simply – despite Baudrillard at
times suggesting this – a matter of compromising between these
two forces, finding somewhere between them. Rather, the true
paradox of time is that it is *both*, at once too fast *and* too slow.
That is to say, it is the things which make time impossible – the
fact that the end is already in the beginning, that we have a
beginning without an end – that also open time up. And it is at
this point, finally, that we return to Baudrillard's first two
hypotheses concerning the end of history: the first that things
are over before they begin; the second that things begin without
ending. As we can see by now, they in fact repeat Baudrillard's
two models or hypotheses concerning time: the first corresponding to cyclical time; the second to linear time. Baudrillard does
not choose between them because fundamentally they are the
same or inseparable from each other. And, as we might also see,
they are hypotheses concerning not simply the end of history

but, taken together, its very possibility. This is why perhaps Baudrillard can call his article both 'The Year 2000 Will Not Take Place' and 'The Year 2000 Has Already Happened'. It is not simply that the proof of the year 2000 having happened is the fact we do not realize it, but that it is the very impossibility of time or history, the year 2000 taking place, which makes it possible. We would say with Zeno that the end of history is impossible, that every moment is the deferral of the end of history, that we never know how we get from one moment to the next; but this only because the end is already in the beginning, every moment of history stands in for the end of history, history has already ended. In a sense, then, we would say that the end of history takes place at once at a real point (although, against Canetti, we could never know where it is), at the very beginning of history (because linear history is only possible because the end is already in the beginning), and never takes place (because, as Zeno says, it is due to this end that it is never achieved, or, as Baudrillard puts it, that we never realize it).

Is not this argument about time precisely also what Baudrillard says about simulation, history as simulation? History is only possible because of the end of history (history is only possible because the events of history are excluded at the beginning), and history leads to the end of history (the end of history takes place because there is too much history). And this end of history is unthinkable because it is either too soon (insofar as we can think it, it has not yet happened) or too late (insofar as it has happened, we are unable to think it); but it is also what *doubles* history, explains how it is possible.[8] 'The Year 2000' is a brilliant analysis not only of the relationship of history to that event which takes place at its beginning and end, but also of time to the now. It shows how history at once excludes this event and stands in for it at every moment. It is a thinking of the simultaneity of the actual and the virtual within systems of simulation. And of time itself as a kind of incessant 'pulsation' between the actual and the virtual, history and its end, the too fast and the too slow. To conclude, this is why, if Baudrillard poses the following question, he cannot himself answer it. Time, history, would be the simultaneity of, the undecidability between the two, the very question itself. It is that impossible choice, as we have tried to demonstrate, that runs throughout his work between the system and its other, between the system increasing and the system turning back on itself. Baudrillard writes at the end of 'The Year 2000':

> Analogically [with the question of the expansion or contraction of the universe], whether our human history is evolving or devolving perhaps depends on the critical mass of humanity. Has the history, the destiny of the species reached the escape velocity necessary to overcome the inertia of the mass? Are we caught, like the galaxies, in an irrevocable movement which draws us away from one another at enormous speed, or is this infinite dispersion destined to come to an end, and the human molecules to draw together following an inverse gravitational movement? Could the human mass, which is increasing all the time, have a pulsation of this kind? ('2000', 27)

Notes

1. Baudrillard will continue this line of argument later in *Consumer Society* in the sections 'Distinction and Conformity' (*CS*, 133–5) and 'Sociometric Compatibility' (*CS*, 271–3). In many ways, *Consumer Society* is a meditation on the collapse of the class-based analysis of Chapin and others and thus on the impossibility of sociometrics.

2. Baudrillard begins *In the Shadow*, as his translators note, by making a number of puns involving the French word '*masse*'. In French, '*faire masse*', for example, means both 'to form an earth', as we say of electricity, and 'to form a majority', as we say of an electoral party (*SSM*, 1). But the point Baudrillard might be trying to make here is that, more than simply allowing metaphor, the masses are themselves metaphoric, the metaphoricity of language in general. Baudrillard speaks of the masses as a kind of 'ground' or 'earth', but as well as being metaphors, these are metaphors of metaphor – which show that our 'ground', our 'earth', is itself only metaphoric. For an excellent analysis of this aspect of Baudrillard's work, see Jean-Marie Berthelot, 'The Masses: From Being to Nothingness' (1986).

3. This simultaneity or 'double strategy' explains Baudrillard's interest in the joke or pun in *In the Shadow*, and his attribution to the masses of a certain 'immanent humour' (*SSM*, 30), 'wit' (*SSM*, 36) or 'irony' (*SSM*, 37). Like the symbolic violence of poetry at the end of *The Mirror of Production* (*MP*, 164–7) or graffiti in *Symbolic Exchange* (*SE*, 76–84), there are two different and opposed signifieds (defiance and conformity) in the one signifier (silence). This

is why in *In the Shadow* Baudrillard raises the 'intolerable hypothesis' that it might be possible to communicate 'outside of the medium of meaning' (*SSM*, 36).

4. There is a beautiful example of this in Woody Allen's film *Zelig*, which Baudrillard uses as an example of conformity (*ED*, 15–16; *Skrien*, 1983–4: 15). In the film, we find out, apparently as a result of Zelig being hypnotized, that his condition of compulsive 'chameleon-like' imitation of those around him was caused by his being embarrassed to admit that he had not read Herman Melville's novel *Moby Dick*. Later on we see Zelig's psychoanalyst, Dr Fletcher, pretend herself not to have read the novel, thus allowing Zelig to be put under hypnosis as a result of him conforming to her as patient. In other words, if her treatment works by her conforming to Zelig in not having read *Moby Dick*, she also could not have known this about him until after he began conforming to her! If in one way she conforms to Zelig, in another way she conforms to nothing, because the very Zelig to whom she conforms comes about only after her.

5. This strategy of deliberately adopting the weaker position in order to turn it into a position of strength, this naming of our limits as a means of overcoming them, is also considered by Michel Serres in 'Knowledge in the Classical Age: La Fontaine and Descartes' (1981). There is an essay which compares the various 'demons' of Descartes, Baudrillard and Serres in relation to this question of naming limits, the limits to naming limits, etc.: Tony Thwaites, 'Miracles: Hot Air and Histories of the Improbable' (1986).

6. For a good essay on this understanding of the 'end' in Baudrillard, see William Bogard, 'Baudrillard, Time and the End' (1994). Kellner himself speaks of this notion of the 'end of history', but fails to grasp that Baudrillard means by this not so much its literal end as the fact that there is more and more history. Thus the solution Kellner offers – to 'provide a historical narrative of such an epochal transformation' (Kellner 1989: 212) – would be itself part of the very problem Baudrillard is analysing.

7. Baudrillard says in *The Perfect Crime* that the 'ultimate is for an idea to disappear as idea to become a thing among things' (*PC*, 100). However, as he also says, it can never entirely do this, there is always a limit, the crime is never perfect, things are never absolutely identical with themselves (*PC*, 2).

8. The final equivalence to be drawn here would be between the year 2000 and the 'now', for like the 'now' the year 2000 would either be too soon (insofar as we can think it, it has not yet happened) or too late (insofar as it has happened, we can no longer think it). We see the same theme subtly reworked in *Fatal Strategies*, where Baudrillard writes:

> What protects us is that, [with regard to the] nuclear holocaust, the event threatens dangerously to deny us all hope of spectacle. *That is why it won't happen.* Humanity can accept its own physical disappearance, but it cannot accept to sacrifice its spectacle (unless it succeeds in finding a spectator in another world). The drive to spectacle is more powerful than the survival instinct, we can count on that. (*FS*, 186)

Conclusion:
Judging Baudrillard in His Own Terms

Baudrillard is undoubtedly a controversial and divisive figure. Opinions about his work vary between the hyperbolic adulation and stylistic imitation of the Canadian Arthur Kroker, who lauds Baudrillard as '*the* postmodern commotion' (Kroker, Kroker and Cook, 1989: 265), to the outright condemnation of the British Marxist Alex Callinicos, who argues that the 'upshot of Baudrillard's analyses is to licence a kind of intellectual dandyism where unsubstantiated theoretical propositions rub shoulders with banal *aperçus*' (1990: 147). In between, there are any number of other critics and theorists like the American sociologist, Sara Schoonmaker, who, while acknowledging Baudrillard's work as 'useful in identifying the digital code as a key part of current processes of social transformation', qualifies this with the caution that it is undermined by the problems of 'technological determinism, formalism and epistemological confusion' (1994: 186). Why do estimations differ so markedly with regard to Baudrillard? Indeed, why is it that with his work, far more than with that of other 'comparable' theorists, there is so much disagreement as to its basic worth? (We would say that with other major contemporary theorists disagreement only occurs *within* the fundamental assumption of the importance and contribution their work makes.) Perhaps it is because Baudrillard, in his seemingly direct reference to contemporary social reality, his apparently non-philosophical stance, poses from the outset much more than those others the question of how to read him, the choice as to whether to assess him by some external standard or in his own terms. Perhaps it is because one of the issues his work raises is the whole problem of how to judge, how to speak critically, in the absence of outside criteria. Opinions of Baudrillard seem to shift dramatically according to whether we agree with his initial premise – that it is necessary to judge both his work and the systems it addresses in their own terms – or not. Before engaging with his work, in the very decision as to how to read it, we seem already to have pre-judged it, made up our mind as to its ultimate value. Baudrillard is symptomatic, we might say, of the whole problem of how to read 'theory'.

Let us take two interpretations of Baudrillard, one external and the other internal, one that judges him in terms of some outside real and the other that judges him in his own terms. The first is by the Dutch American studies scholar, Hans Bertens, in his book *The Idea of the Postmodern: A History*. In *The Idea of the Postmodern*, Bertens puts forward a series of readings of some of the leading proponents of the 'postmodern', amongst them Jürgen Habermas, Jean-François Lyotard, Richard Rorty and Fredric Jameson, comparing their various approaches throughout. In his chapter 'Antithetical Radicalisms: Richard Rorty and Jean Baudrillard', Bertens at first summarizes Baudrillard's work, with particular emphasis on his notions of the 'code' and simulation, before offering the following diagnosis, citing Mark Poster's Introduction to his volume of Baudrillard's *Selected Writings*:

> He [Baudrillard] fails to define his major terms, such as the code; his writing style is hyperbolic and declarative, often lacking sustained, systematic analysis when it is appropriate; he totalizes his insights, refusing to qualify or delimit his claims. He writes about particular experiences, television

> images, as if nothing else in society mattered, extrapolating a bleak view of the world from that limited base. He ignores contradictory evidence such as the many benefits afforded by the new media, for example, by providing vital information to the populace (the Vietnam War) and counteracting parochialism with humanizing images of foreigners. The instant, worldwide availability of information has changed human society forever, probably for the good. (1995: 156–7)

Bertens's solution to this, as the title of his chapter indicates, is to put Baudrillard together with the American pragmatist philosopher Richard Rorty, so that 'Rorty's somewhat myopic optimism will be tempered by Baudrillard's grim analysis of the post-modern condition while Baudrillard's soaring claims will be seen in the perspective of Rorty's down-home insistence on the actual' (1995: 144–5).

What is wrong with this? It is not that it is largely critical of Baudrillard. Criticisms of his work always can and should be made. It is rather that it does not question its own assumptions about Baudrillard, that before making these allegations another series of questions must be asked. How would Baudrillard respond to these charges? How – as with any text – has his work already responded to them? That is, it is not enough to accuse Baudrillard of being 'hyperbolic and declarative' without also asking whether this is necessarily a bad thing, what Baudrillard's reasons are for this. It is not enough to oppose some empirical reality to his theory – the 'many benefits afforded by the new media', the 'worldwide availability of information' – without asking what Baudrillard's theory itself says about the relationship of reality to theory. (And, of course, Bertens's and Poster's supposedly factual information is just as much unsupported assertion as anything Baudrillard himself says. *Is* information necessarily beneficial? *Is* it truly worldwide? And this is not even to consider whether Baudrillard's theory is in fact proven or refuted by this spread of 'beneficial', 'worldwide' information.) Finally, what exactly is at stake in Bertens somehow fusing Baudrillard with Rorty? To produce a more 'balanced' theory, poised sensibly between 'optimism' and 'pessimism', 'soaring claims' and 'down-home insistence on the actual'? But why *should* theory be balanced in this way? What do such qualities of temperament as optimism and pessimism have to do with theory? What could it mean to join such seemingly opposed or incompatible theories as Baudrillard's and Rorty's? What is to be achieved by it? What do they have in common? What allows them to be compared in this way? In not considering any of these questions, we can see Bertens's claims about Baudrillard to be themselves 'hyperbolic and declarative', those accusations he makes against Baudrillard to apply before all else to himself.

Now let us look at an example of an internal reading of Baudrillard's work, one written with an awareness of these sorts of problems, the difficulty of approaching or attempting to judge him. It is an essay by the Australian cultural critic Meaghan Morris entitled 'Room 101 or A Few Worst Things in the World', originally published in the 1984 collection *Seduced and Abandoned: The Baudrillard Scene* and later reprinted in her book *The Pirate's Fiancée: Feminism, Reading, Postmodernism*. It is still perhaps the best piece written on Baudrillard. In it, Morris begins by admitting that, like the fatally conforming objects he himself analyses, Baudrillard's work already responds to any criticism made of it so that in a way the critic attacking him only ends up speaking of him- or herself: 'Baudrillard approaches his object(s) with proper humility and resignation: so, woe to the one who would in turn approach the malignity, the cynicism, the brilliance of a Baudrillard text with a banal lack of decorum' (1984: 94). It is not therefore some simple notion of the real that Morris holds against Baudrillard, for she knows that this real is precisely only to be seen through him. Rather, she wants to think what is excluded by this very match between the world and his theory, the way everything only becomes an example for or exemplary of it. She wants to think why what begins as a description of the world ends up describing only itself. Morris writes:

> If for Baudrillard narration is not impossible, but rather an ideal condition which theory might strive to attain, it is nevertheless the case that throughout his work the fable always comes to supplement and to repeat description; and

that both fable and description are redundancies multiplied in, by and for the demonstration of a discourse demonstrating its own inevitability. This has always been the absorbing fascination of the theory of simulation: it offers a universe, an inexhaustible, infinite world of examples, exemplary matter, for the citing of the theory itself. From obesity to terrorism, from the clone to the handicapped, it can discourse upon anything at all and always say the same thing. (1984: 112)

But Morris does not simply leave it at that, which she admits would be both 'ungenerous and inexact' (1984: 112). She goes on to speak of the way that – as in the third order of simulacra – there is in Baudrillard's work a dream of something that is not merely an effect of its discourse, that while appearing to resemble it in fact only conforms to it: 'some arch Object, some wonderful and transcendent Thing that might never succumb to hype, but rather lure it along, exhaust it, stand ironic and indifferent as hype spends itself in its ecstasy of annihilation' (1984: 114). And it is this that produces the particular structure of Baudrillard's work for Morris: the fact that it speaks endlessly about its own inability to speak; that those objects it says are always beyond it, only conform to it, do not bring it to an end but on the contrary incite it; that where there is 'most delight in a Baudrillard who declares that "the real" no longer exists, there is most admiration for a writer who at last describes the way things *really* are' (1984: 95). She concludes:

So Baudrillard's discourse is garrulous about the silence of an object which might still somehow speak: so it vaunts the powers of enigma and seductive senselessness, while creating a most severe and rigorous and predictive allegorical mode of reading and writing [. . .]. We ourselves have made sure there is no way out: and turning, as we confirm on every page that nightmare absence of Things, we see the sign of our own dear despair approaching – with the assurance that in this place, whatever the question, we will know the answer already. (1984: 114–15)

Morris offers a brilliant analysis of Baudrillard here, but if we could differ from her it would be to say that perhaps her argument is unduly negative, apocalyptic, like the very Baudrillard she speaks of (and throughout her text, in an admittedly ironic way, she interweaves excerpts from Orwell's novel *Nineteen Eighty-Four*, the date of its original appearance).[1] For we must ask first of all: is this problem of description peculiar to Baudrillard? Do we not have the sense with all major theorists that the real only exists as an endless series of examples, as material for their arguments? But beyond this what meaning could the real have, what could come from it, except within a theory, even Morris's own? For if we might point to a certain inconsistency in Morris, it is that she says at once – and both are true, but she does not think through the consequences of this – that Baudrillard 'always says the same thing' about the real and that his theory 'ever pursues' (1984: 114) itself through this real, is never entirely able to grasp itself. We would say that the real – the very real Morris is trying to speak of – *is* this inability of Baudrillard's system to close upon itself, an inability that it does not itself see. This is why it is so important to read Baudrillard closely, which Morris does but which so few writers on Baudrillard do. It is exactly in the inconsistencies, contradictions and illogicalities of his argument that we might see what the real, the resistance of the real, might mean, why a theoretical text can never become totally self-consistent. It is this Baudrillard holds against the systems he analyses and it is this we must think in any estimation of his work. We merely begin the process here when we look at the equivocations that occur at certain moments of his texts: the difficulty of the place of the analyst of simulation; the impossibility of mastering seduction; the chance that the fatal object conforms even to Baudrillard's own analysis of it. This is why Baudrillard's theory might be that 'absolute commodity' (1984: 114) Morris speaks of – and we have tried to show this – because it cannot simply be 'used' or 'applied' by anyone, even Baudrillard himself.

It is only in this sense that it is meaningful to ask the questions Bertens poses, that we might use 'other' criteria to judge Baudrillard's work. (This is why, if that external reading does not see the possibility of this internal reading, this internal reading already sees and accounts for that external reading.

The 'indifference' of that external reading, as in seduction, is doubled by, only possible because of, that internal reading [*BL*, 126].[2]) For instance, in the light of this internal reading, what is the real for Baudrillard? It is neither merely outside nor inside the system that describes it, but the very difference between the system and what it tries to describe, what at once allows the system to resemble the real and what must forever be excluded for the system to resemble the real. We see this real in the form of waste in Chapter 1, the medium of exchange in Chapter 2 and the masses in Chapter 3. What is the future of social action and politics after Baudrillard? They must be re-imagined or re-invented on the basis of an always virtual real that is excluded from all systems, including Baudrillard's own. It would necessitate a certain politics or ethics of the unrepresentable. What is the effect of the fact that no system can ever entirely resemble the world, that something is always missing from it? What does it mean that, if in one way we can and must say what is excluded from our modern systems of simulation, in another way we cannot? In the name of what would we speak against them? These are the kinds of questions that must henceforth guide politics in the light of Baudrillard's work. And, finally, how are we to understand his sources and his commonality with other thinkers? Again, if in one way we can see the influence of others on Baudrillard, his project shifting in response to them, in another way this is not true. Baudrillard's argument remains the same throughout all of his work; if he takes up the ideas of others, it is only insofar as they are saying what he already is. We cannot compare great or important philosophical systems because each creates its own real, determines the very standards or criteria by which we must judge it. Or to return to the question of how the real might be reconceptualized here, we might compare them only insofar as there arises within each this same problem of non-closure, the real as the inability to become entirely self-consistent. If there is a real they share, it is a real only *within* each of them, a limit to each of them that is the real.

We might pause at this point, for what is raised here is perhaps the ultimate context in which to see Baudrillard's work

– a context that would at once require further elaboration and
that would be itself challenged by Baudrillard. As we suggest,
the crucial issue for Baudrillard – precisely that which is not
addressed by merely external readings of his work – is this
question of closure. Baudrillard does not directly challenge the
systems he analyses because they are closed, have no other.
And we do not directly challenge Baudrillard because his work
too is closed. But when did this question of closure first arise in
thought? Perhaps with Hegel. It was with Hegel's dialectic that
thought was first understood as working through its other, that
if it was only possible because of its other, this other was only
possible because of it. In a sense, then, there could be no
simple other to Hegel's *Phenomenology* because any other we
spoke of would only be that which it has already spoken of,
that which has already been accounted for by it. And Hegel's
was perhaps the first philosophy that consciously understood
itself as offering an explanation for everything, the last possible
thought of the world. The problem for philosophers after Hegel,
therefore – it is the very problem we have looked at in
Baudrillard's work – is how to think an other to this system
that has no other, in which otherness is its very object. The
solution is not simply the refutation or posing of alternatives to
Hegel, but a thinking of what is excluded to allow this all-
inclusiveness, that other excluded to ensure it has no other.
These other philosophers saw in Hegel someone who worked
by doubling – for we never see the completed dialectic as such,
nothing is changed by it but everything is explained by it – and
who therefore could only be doubled. They did not simply
oppose Hegel, but attempted to be as it were more Hegelian
than Hegel, argued he was right but only for reasons he could
not see. For Kierkegaard, Hegel was right but only because of a
kind of subjective irony. For Nietzsche, Hegel was right but
only because of the Eternal Return. For Bataille, Hegel was
right but only because of death, laughter and sacrifice. Each of
these thinkers speaks in the name of an always excluded
'nothing' against Hegel. They do not simply offer a new thought
– for Hegel's is the last possible thought – but a reflection upon
this last thought, a thinking of this last thought, and thus a

thought after that. (In a way like 'The Year 2000', every thought is henceforth the last thought, both stands in for and defers this last thought.)

We would say that it was perhaps that group of thinkers called post-structuralist who were the first to think *this*, who first saw the advance of knowledge not simply as a matter of empirical argument and refutation, but bound up with the closure of thought, not so much a thinking of new thought as new reasons for the old thought, not so much the end of thought as what is excluded to allow it to reach this end and thus why it is always open to a certain future. If we say there is anything in common to the various thinkers called post-structuralist, we would say that it is this notion of thought as *doubling*, as continuing even in the absence of any external standards of judgement outside of the world and its systems. We might think here of Derrida and his project of deconstructing presence when for him there is nothing outside of it, when there is only the experience of presence and the present of experience. We might think of Lyotard and his attempt to speak against Capital when for him Capital has no limit, to institute a certain justice when for him there is no final value on the basis of which to adjudicate. We might think of Deleuze and Foucault and their efforts to devise a liberatory politics when for them there is no outside to power and reterritorialization, when all direct resistance or opposition to power only returns us to its circuits, leads to its extension.[3] We might think of Irigaray and her attempt to think the feminine when for her there is no outside to masculine logic, when all attempts to speak of woman's desire would fall back into masculine systems of representation. In each, it is not a matter simply of proposing an alternative to the system under investigation, but rather of pushing it to its limit. It is at this point, they speculate, that the system will turn against itself, that a certain outside to the system will open up or will show itself to have made the system possible from the very beginning. In each, there is a certain doubling hypothesis, which at once explains why the system they oppose is in place and is the only possible one and why it is finally impossible – impossible because, while it is predicated on being self-enclosed, able to account for itself, it is finally staked on a principle outside of it. In each, we see a new notion of criticism, one that works not by description, evidence, enunciation, but by prescription, doubling, annunciation. Each attempts to devise a series of statements that the world can only follow (and follow even when it does not appear to follow). There *is différance*. There *is* the sublime or unpresentable. There *is* resistance or deterritorialization. There *is* woman.

This, we would argue, is the proper 'context' for Baudrillard. It is a thought that takes place, as Baudrillard says in *The Transparency of Evil*, at the end of our modernity, at the end of the assurance of our own proper destiny or meaning. (The Enlightenment has both failed or collapsed and been realized, leaving us to wonder what to do next, how critical thought can continue to operate in the wake of a fully realized utopia [*TE*, 4].) It is a thought that seeks to judge in the absence of the Grand Narratives of Truth, Progress, Reason, Humanity, etc. It seeks to judge when there are only the immanent standards of the world. It is not to forgo the necessity of criticism, of thinking from somewhere else – those who characterize Baudrillard as simply passive, fatalistic, nihilistic (including Baudrillard himself at times) are wrong – but rather asks how this is to be done within capitalism's self-legitimating, self-authorizing systems, systems which precisely set the horizons for their own evaluation.[4] It is only by grasping Baudrillard in this way that we might ask profound questions of him. It is only those critics who admit the necessity and limitations of an internal reading, think the relationship of this internal reading to any external reading – both Baudrillard's of the systems he analyses and of Baudrillard's own work – who are truly able to read Baudrillard at all. It is in fact paradoxically only on the basis of this internal reading that we might think the relevance of Baudrillard's work to other disciplines, for example sociology. It is after it that we might ask such questions as: what are the limits of sociology as a discipline? How can sociology think these limits and how can it not? How might sociology re-invent itself as a thinking of representation, of that difference at the heart of representation?

These are the questions Baudrillard asks in his work, but it is not a matter of simply asking them again or re-applying the answers Baudrillard gives. Rather, it is to realize that properly to ask these questions today is to transform or to produce an unrecognizable Baudrillard, to read 'Baudrillard against himself'. We would be most Baudrillardian in sociology not in merely following him but in discovering or inventing a certain 'Baudrillard effect' within it, something that repeats the internal logic of his work but within the internal logic of sociology (which shows that neither logic is simply internal, but external in a different way).[5] This is in the end how great or powerful thinkers live on, not so much because of some pre-determined body of doctrine they set out but because they offer rules for their own transformation, understand themselves as only an effect of their own reading, translation, seduction, doubling. As Baudrillard says in response to a question from the multi-media critic Nicholas Zurbrugg, reminding him of his notorious statement that 'It would be a very good idea publicly to sacrifice a post-modern philosopher': 'Why not! Yes!' (*BL*, 168–9)

Notes

1. For a reading of Baudrillard that is indebted to Morris, but without her sense of the difficulties of critiquing him, the necessity for an internal reading, see Richard Allen, 'Critical Theory and the Paradox of Modernist Discourse', (1987).

2. For analyses of Baudrillard's work that see the difficulties it poses to merely external readings of it, the way that it would contest the terms in which they are posed (without necessarily grasping the precise relationship between internal and external readings), see Stuart Sim, '"The Text Must Scoff at Meaning": Baudrillard and the Politics of Simulation and Hyperreality' in *Beyond Aesthetics* (1992); and Chris Rojek and Bryan S. Turner, 'Regret Baudrillard?' in *Forget Baudrillard?* (1993).

3. We realize that we are arguing here that Baudrillard and Foucault and Deleuze are in fact saying the same thing. Though we do not offer a reading of it here, we would say that after Baudrillard's 'Forget Foucault' we can see their respective bodies of work as 'identical'. For instance, we would say that what Foucault means by 'pleb' (1979: 52) and Deleuze by 'schizo' is what Baudrillard means by the masses, that for Foucault and Deleuze too power works by a certain seduction, fundamentally does not exist. Thus, against Alan Schrift in

his *Nietzsche's French Legacy* (1995: 138), we would say that Baudrillard, Foucault and Deleuze are saying the same thing, *but only after Baudrillard has written*. Baudrillard is well aware that the ultimate fate of all critiques is that we can see the original already saying what the other says it should be saying. For a good analysis of the Baudrillard and Foucault 'debate', see Calvin Thomas, 'Baudrillard's Seduction of Foucault' (1992).

4. This is the problem Lyotard addresses in his *The Postmodern Condition: A Report on Knowledge*, 1984.

5. For good attempts to re-read Baudrillard in specifically sociological terms, see Barry Smart, 'On the Disorder of Things: Sociology, Postmodernity and the "End of the Social"' (1990); William Bogard, 'Sociology in the Absence of the Social: The Significance of Baudrillard for Contemporary Thought' (1987); Chris Rojek, 'Baudrillard and Politics' (1993), and Dean and Juliet Flower MacCannell, 'Social Class in Postmodernity: Simulacrum or Return of the Real?' (1993).

References

Allen, Richard (1987) 'Critical Theory and the Paradox of Modernist Discourse', *Screen*, 28 (2): 69–85

Baudrillard, Jean (1987) 'The Year 2000 Has Already Happened', in A. Kroker and M. Kroker (eds), *Body Invaders: Body Sex in America* (Montreal: New World Publishing) pp. 35–44

Baudrillard, Jean (1983–4) 'Zelig', *Skrien*, 132 (3): 15

Baudrillard, Jean (1988a) *America* (London: Verso)

Baudrillard, Jean (1988b) 'Beyond the Vanishing Point of Art', in P. Taylor (ed.), *Post-Pop Art* (Cambridge, MA: MIT Press) pp. 171–89

Baudrillard, Jean (1995) *The Gulf War Did Not Take Place* (Sydney: Power Publishing)

Bertens, Hans (1995) *The Idea of the Postmodern: A History* (London: Routledge)

Berthelot, Jean-Marie (1986) 'The Masses: From Being to Nothingness' ['Les masses: de l'être au néant'], in J. Zylberberg (ed.), *Masses and Postmodernity [Masses et postmodernité]* (Paris: Méridiens Klincksieck) pp. 179–94

Bogard, William (1987) 'Sociology in the Absence of the Social: The Significance of Baudrillard for Contemporary Thought', *Philosophy and Social Criticism*, 13 (3): 227–42

Bogard, William (1994) 'Baudrillard, Time and the End', in D. Kellner (ed.), *Baudrillard: A Critical Reader* (Oxford: Blackwell) pp. 313–33

Borges, Jorge Luis (1981) *Labyrinths* (Harmondsworth: Penguin)

Callinicos, Alex (1990) *Against Postmodernism: A Marxist Critique* (New York: St Martin's Press)

Chang, Briankle (1986) 'Mass Media, Mass Mediation: Baudrillard's Implosive

Critique of Modern Mass-Mediated Culture', *Current Perspectives in Social Theory*, 17: 157–81

Chapin, F. Stuart (1935) *Contemporary American Institutions: A Sociological Analysis* (New York: Harpers)

Chen, Kuan-Hsing (1987) 'The Masses and the Media: Baudrillard's Implosive Postmodernism', *Theory, Culture & Society*, 4 (1): 71–88

Cook, Deborah (1994) 'Symbolic Exchange in Hyperreality', in D. Kellner (ed.), *Baudrillard: A Critical Reader* (Oxford: Blackwell) pp. 150–67

Derrida, Jacques (1981) *Dissemination* (London: The Athlone Press)

Descartes, René (1977) *Philosophical Writings* (London: Nelson's University Paperbacks)

Dunn, Robert (1991) 'Postmodernism, Populism, Mass Culture and the Avant-Garde', *Theory, Culture & Society*, 8 (1): 111–26

Faye, Jean-Pierre (1985) 'The Infernal Left' ['La gauche infernale'], *Change International*, 3: 5–6

Foucault, Michel (1977a) *The Order of Things: An Archaeology of the Human Sciences* (London: Tavistock)

Foucault, Michel (1977b) *Language, Counter-Memory, Practice* (Oxford: Blackwell)

Foucault, Michel (1979) 'Power and Strategies', in M. Morris and P. Patton (eds), *Michel Foucault: Power, Truth, Strategy* (Sydney: Feral Publications) pp. 49–58

Gallop, Jane (1989) 'French Theory and the Seduction of Feminism', in A. Jardine and P. Smith (eds), *Men in Feminism* (London: Routledge) pp. 111–15

Gane, Mike (1991a) *Baudrillard: Critical and Fatal Theory* (London: Routledge)

Gane, Mike (1991b) *Baudrillard's Bestiary: Baudrillard and Culture* (London: Routledge)

Genosko, Gary (1994) *Baudrillard and Signs: Signification Ablaze* (London: Routledge)

Goshorn, Keith (1994) 'Valorizing "the Feminine" while Rejecting Feminism? – Baudrillard's Feminist Provocations', in D. Kellner (ed.), *Baudrillard: A Critical Reader* (Oxford: Blackwell) pp. 257–91

Hughes, Robert (1992) *Nothing if Not Critical: Essays on Art and Artists* (New York: Penguin)

Hultkrans, Andrew (1997) 'Crap Shoot', *Artforum*, 35 (5): 21–2

Irigaray, Luce (1980) 'Woman is Nothing and That is Her Power' ['La Femme n'est rien et c'est là sa puissance'], *Histoires d'elles*, 21: 3

Johnson, Barbara (1977) 'The Frame of Reference: Poe, Lacan, Derrida', *Yale French Studies*, 55–6: 457–505

Kellner, Douglas (1989) *Jean Baudrillard: From Marxism to Postmodernism and Beyond* (Stanford: Stanford University Press)

Kierkegaard, Søren (1971) *Either/Or*, Vol. I (Princeton, NJ: Princeton University Press)

Kroker, Arthur, Kroker, Marilouise and Cook, David (1989) *Panic Encyclopaedia: The Definitive Guide to Postmodernism* (London: Macmillan)

Langlois, Simon (1986) 'Consumption, ways of life and the explosion of the masses', ['Consommation, modes de vie et éclatement de la masse'], in J. Zylberberg (ed.), *Masses and Postmodernity [Masses et postmodernité]* (Paris: Méridiens Klincksieck) pp. 105–16

Levin, Charles (1996) *Jean Baudrillard: A Study in Cultural Metaphysics* (Hemel Hempstead: Prentice Hall)

Lyotard, Jean-François (1993) *Libidinal Economy* (Bloomington: Indiana University Press)

Morris, Meaghan (1984) 'Room 101 Or A Few Worst Things In The World', in A. Frankovits (ed.), *Seduced and Abandoned: The Baudrillard Scene* (Sydney: Stonemoss Services) pp. 91–117

MacCannell, Dean and MacCannell, Juliet Flower (1993) 'Social Class in Postmodernity: Simulacrum or Return of the Real?', in C. Rojek and B.S. Turner (eds), *Forget Baudrillard* (London: Routledge) pp. 124–45

Norris, Christopher (1990) *What's Wrong with Postmodernism?* (London: Prentice Hall)

Norris, Christopher (1992) *Uncritical Theory: Postmodernism, Intellectuals and the Gulf War* (London: Lawrence and Wishart)

Pefanis, Julian (1991) *Heterology and the Postmodern: Bataille, Baudrillard and Lyotard* (Sydney: Allen & Unwin)

Plant, Sadie (1993) 'Baudrillard's Woman: The Eve of Seduction', in C. Rojek and B.S. Turner (eds), *Forget Baudrillard?* (London: Routledge) pp. 88–106

Plato (1875) *The Dialogues of Plato*, Vol. II (London: Clarendon Press)

Rickels, Laurence (1993) 'Opportunistic Diagnosis', *Artforum*, 31 (10): 11–12

Rojek, Chris (1993) 'Baudrillard and Politics', in C. Rojek and B.S. Turner (eds), *Forget Baudrillard* (London: Routledge) pp. 107–23

Rojek, Chris and Turner, B.S. (1993) 'Regret Baudrillard?', in C. Rojek and B.S. Turner (eds), *Forget Baudrillard* (London: Routledge) pp. ix–xviii

Ross, Andrew (1989) 'Baudrillard's Bad Attitude', in D. Hunter (ed.), *Seduction and Theory* (Urbana: University of Illinois Press) pp. 214–25

Schoonmaker, Sara (1994) 'Capitalism and the Code: A Critique of Baudrillard', in D. Kellner (ed.), *Baudrillard: A Critical Reader* (Oxford: Blackwell) pp. 168–88

Schrift, Alan (1995) *Nietzsche's French Legacy: A Genealogy of Poststructuralism* (London: Routledge)

Serres, Michel (1981) *Hermes: Language, Science, Philosophy* (Baltimore: Johns Hopkins University Press)

Sim, Stuart (1992) *Beyond Aesthetics: Confrontations with Poststructuralism and Postmodernism* (Hemel Hempstead: Harvester Wheatsheaf)

Smart, Barry (1990) 'On the Disorder of Things: Postmodernity and the "End of the Social"', *Sociology*, 24 (3): 397–416

Stevenson, Nick (1995) *Understanding Media Cultures* (London: Sage Publications)

Tarter, Jim (1991) 'Baudrillard and the Problematics of Post-New Left Media Theory', *American Journal of Semiotics*, 8 (4): 155–71

Thomas, Calvin (1992) 'Baudrillard's Seduction of Foucault', in W. Chaloupka and W. Stearns (eds), *Jean Baudrillard: The Disappearance of Art and Politics* (London: Macmillan) pp. 131–45

Thwaites, Tony (1986) 'Miracles: Hot Air and Histories of the Improbable', in E.A. Grosz, T. Threadgold, D. Kelly, A. Cholodenko and E. Colless (eds), *Futur*Fall: Excursions into Postmodernity* (Sydney: Power Publishing) pp. 82–96

Turner, Bryan S. (1987) 'A Note on Nostalgia', *Theory, Culture & Society*, 4 (1): 147–56

Valente, Joseph (1985) 'Hall of Mirrors: Baudrillard on Marx', *Diacritics*, 15 (2): 54–65

Weber, Samuel (1985) 'Afterword', in J-F. Lyotard, *Just Gaming* (Manchester: Manchester University Press) pp. 101–20

Wills, David (1995) *Prostheses* (Stanford: Stanford University Press)

Žižek, Slavoj (1993) *Tarrying with the Negative: Kant, Hegel and the Critique of Ideology* (Durham, NC: Duke University Press)

Subject Index

Name Index